From Pain to Absolute Peace

A Journey to Remember

My Memoir

Mila Gatchalian

Dedication

I write this book to my sons Paul Capulong and Michael Capulong. You both inspire me, give me hope, and show me the meaning of love. I am so proud of you two.

Thank you for giving me the will to live and showing me the way to survive.

I will love you forever!

Preface

I am human, born with every weakness humanly possible within me; what am I to do when the devil comes along?

"I can do all things through Christ who strengthens me," Paul said in (Philippines 4:13).

Strength; it's a concept that not many can grasp. While some may believe that strength is purely physical, it's important to know that there are more ways to gain it; sometimes more than once. That's what Christ does – every challenge you face, the nostalgia you feel, and the depression you land in, Christ is there to strengthen you. It's your decision to let him in.

This is my memoir—a story of hope, strength, and life in all its sad, hopeless reality. However, no sadness remains, and so I write this as a message to all the women. It doesn't matter if you're from a broken home, or in a broken marriage, or are empathetic toward anyone who is in these circumstances – you will survive.

I also write this to the sons and daughters who have forgotten peace in their own homes. Remember; there will be peace; you must never give up. Where there are problems, there is always a solution, and God will provide that for you. The key is patience.

There's no 'easiness' in God's way. It may be perfect, ideal, and "natural." However, it needs hard work. When you consider God's way, you may find that, someday, you still may have to work at it. Just because something is right doesn't mean it's easy. Someday you need a little more strength than others. But remember that God is always there to help. It is something that my mother and grandmother always reminded me of when I could not find peace.

"Be courageous and religious.'

It means fast and pray fervently!

Don't give up. Don't give in. Hold on. The blessing is on your way.

Acknowledgments

To the loving memory of my parents, Marcelo and Teofila Gatchalian, and my grandmother, Anicia Marasigan. You have taught me to believe that "I can do all things through Christ, who strengthens me." (Philippians 4:13). Thank you for showing me the way of Christ. You have shown me unconditional love and have always been a source of guidance. Thank you for always reminding me to be humble at heart.

To my family, friends, brokers, and clients in Real Estate. You've helped me in every possible way and have given me the support to reach all of my goals. You've shown me what true friendship is all about. If it weren't for all of you, I would have never become the longtime recipient of the HRRA Circle of Excellence. Thank you for everything.

To all my students in public and private schools in the Philippines and in the United States, I have been blessed with the opportunity to have taught each and every one of you. I am so proud of all of you for becoming such wonderful people.

One of the gifts of being a Benedictine Oblate is the opportunity to extend God's love to parishes, churches, and civic organizations. I got to experience the love and joy that Christ promised when I facilitated the Bible Study at St. Gregory church in Virginia Beach and again at St. Gerard Majella church in Los Angeles, California. I will never forget the immense gratification I experienced on those days.

Thank you all for your loving support. I am so grateful for all the people who have helped me in my journey of making this book a possibility and successful. I have written strong messages, especially for you all in this book to pass on to.

Remember to never give up. Be courageous and always have God and Jesus in your hearts.

Contents

Page Left Blank Intentionally

Introduction

A happy marriage is built on honesty and trust. It is built on keeping an open line of communication and respect, with the former ranking higher, even when compared to love. Very much like the rest, I always had a different plan in life. My mind was always full of hopes and dreams, and my vision of marriage was always different. Thirty-six years into my marriage, though, I realized that I had left those hopes and visions far behind. Nothing was as I imagined it.

Pol and I were, for lack of a better word, the ideal example of a functional marriage. How else could we have made our marriage last thirty-six years? It's no wonder that my decision to separate from Pol came as a surprise to everyone in my life, including Pol, my ex-husband.

Beneath the perfect exterior, however, we were in hell. Pol had successfully managed to make my children and my lives a nightmare. Regardless of all of that, I hope that he, too, finds real happiness. I pray he finds the same kind of joy that I have uncovered ever since our separation.

As a mother, I have always placed my sons before my own needs, even emotionally. I do not rely on fate when it comes to my sons' well-being. I love them very much. They are my priority in life!

1

Do not conform yourself to this age but be transformed by the renewal of your mind, that you may discern what is the will of God, what is good and pleasing and perfect. Romans 12:2

Love at First Sight!

Life doesn't wait for anyone. I didn't! Even after thirty-six years, I managed to move on. Sometimes, I replay the life events in my head and wonder what the right word to express the meaning of my life is. Pondering over my past often leads me to have self-blaming thoughts and emotions. I want to cry in frustration because I know I am all to blame. However, my eyes feel so dehydrated that I can't even cry anymore. It is even more exasperating because it feels as if my ability to express the hurt I feel deep inside has been taken away.

What is the first thought that comes to your mind when you hear the word "marriage"?

I have often heard people calling their life a roller-coaster ride, full of ups and downs and turns and twists. However, when I think about my life and its struggles, I believe that the roller coaster is not the right term for my life, at least. Because even a roller coaster ride has some easy turns and moves, but my life has only been full of nerve-wracking challenges ever since I got married.

Perhaps, happiness, a new beginning, love, romance, attachment, family, care, compassion, and so forth. Right?

Well, this is not true in everyone's case. For some people, especially women, marriage proves to be a horrific turn of events.

But let me tell you, no woman knows what she's walking into when she's getting married even if she knows the man she's letting into her life. Knowing someone before you marry them doesn't guarantee you a happy life. It just makes you more miserable afterward that you couldn't recognize the kind of person he was when you had the chance to judge him, free of an obligation to stand by him.

I had that chance, but I was one of the very few girls who were never interested in getting married. Yes, I had a different plan in life, and yet I ended up in a thirty-six-year-long marriage that didn't quite give me what I had dreamed of.

You'd be surprised to know this, but I had always wanted to become a nun. As a Catholic, born in a religious family, my entire concentration had been on the Church. I was a regular attendee, and I so wished to serve the Lord for the rest of my life.

Even in my high school years, I was never the type of girl every other girl wanted to be. I never wanted to be someone who was popular among boys. I kept to myself, and I stayed focused on my goal of becoming a nun.

What I didn't know was that fate had chosen entirely different for me. However, you wouldn't believe how it all started for me. It was like I was living a fairy tale, even filled with appropriate villains where needed.

I had just turned fourteen years old and stepped into my junior year at high school when I began to notice a quiet, nice looking guy in my class. His name was Pol. He was shy. He barely spoke to anyone, and he looked okay for me in respect. I know because he went on to become my husband for thirty-six years of my life!

When I saw him for the first time noticing me, I didn't make much of it. He was also a relative of mine. Our mothers were third-generation cousins, so we often see each other on Christmas and Holidays. On such occasions, I often found him looking for an excuse to place himself beside me.

He was already 5 feet, 8 inches tall, and handsome. I was young and beautiful myself.

We could have made a great couple, except I didn't think so. I had no interest in marrying anyone, so I barely paid any attention to him.

He, on the other hand, was smitten. For him, it was love at first sight! He admired me, and he looked up to me. He thought I was smarter than him. And despite that, he tried to reach me once or twice but snuck away as soon as I had his attention. His behavior made me think he was just too shy to speak to me.

High school came to an end, and he never managed to convey his feelings to me. Though I knew, he was still interested. In our college years, we were in different programs. He had taken architecture as a major, and I had opted for education as a major. We knew what each of us was doing. But he never had the courage to just walk up to me and tell me what he wanted from me.

I, on the other hand, was dedicated fully to my goal. Soon, he began sending other classmates to me with his messages and letters. I found out about the letters after a very long time. At the time, he had been giving the letters to a boy who was also interested in me. He never gave me any of his letters.

Oblivious of his attraction, I went about my business.

I had taken a higher road, a higher calling in life, and I had no intention of deviating from it all until I was literally forced into changing my mind.

Through all my pain and misery, God was all I remembered. I couldn't see anyone else who could get through to me except the Lord, and I know today that I was accurate. At the time, I had been doubtful of this. I had been led astray by others into believing that you can't live your life just by your love for God. You need more. And I believed that no matter how briefly.

A huge part of this belief came from the measures he took to get my attention. When we were in our third year in college, he came to me and asked me out at lunch. I heard his request but didn't say anything to him.

What I didn't know was that this was probably the last time I would see him for a very long time. He had applied at the US Navy, and he had got in!

At that time and in the conditions we had been living in, it had been a tremendous opportunity for him. Yet, he had found it in his heart to go so far away from everyone he loved, just to accomplish his dream. I was happy for him until, one day, he complicated my life.

What he had achieved had been unthinkable, but what he did next shocked us all. At that time, letters used to go to my father first, as he was the head of the mail delivery department in town. He came back home with a letter from him. It said only one thing, "If you don't answer, I will not be back and will not be seen anymore."

I knew what he meant by that. Until this time, I had not paid any attention to his attraction towards me. I had not given it a thought, and I had not responded to his indications that he loved me. I had not even gone to see him before he had left. Now, he wanted me to respond to his unrequited love.

As we were cousins, my family thought we were just close friends, and they let it go. But then he made his attraction public and sent a postcard to his mother. She came to our house and showed it to us. It had the same threatening message, "I won't be home anymore if Mila will not answer my message."

Everyone had become quite worried about him, and I finally answered him.

I succeeded in caring for him when I expected the least. And finally, we became friends. The journey of the next thirty-six years of my life began the moment I wrote back to him. I gave him a place in my heart. For so long, I had kept it reserved for the Lord, and yet when he opened up about what he wanted, I did too, and I began to care for him.

2

Justice will bring about peace; right will produce calm and security. Isaiah 32:17-18

Love or Tricks?

The first time I wrote to him, I had been nervous. I didn't know how he would react. I had no idea how I would react when I received his second letter, but before I knew it, we were friends.

It turned out that being his friend was easy. All I had to do was write back to him. As a girl who had always wanted to embrace the Church and dedicate myself to the Lord, I discovered that I was quite good at being his friend.

There were days when the war depressed him. There were times when he wanted it all to end. The only source of any satisfaction he had was when Mila wrote to him. At least that's what he kept saying in his letters back to her.

Before I realized it, I had grown really close to him. And then he began visiting me when he had the chance. For quite a few days, his ship had been docked in Japan. From there, it was easier for him to visit home.

As soon as he came into town, he brought a huge celebration with him. He was celebrated at home like a hero as he was in the Navy. And he himself enjoyed the attention. He invited our former classmates to our house and threw a party for us all.

We spent three long years this way, loving and caring for each other. By this time, I had begun to believe everything between us was real. We were meant to be with each other. However, after a few days, his family began playing tricks to get us married as quickly as possible.

The whole rush over this marriage was because of the fact that Pol was being posted to Monterey, California. He stayed in our hometown for 45 days so he could sort out several things before leaving for America. I learned later that one of those things was getting married to me.

I began to understand everything when his elder sister showed up at my school suddenly. She had brought Pol along with her. At first, I didn't understand what they were up to. The whole school had erupted with excitement upon their arrival. Most people knew that he and I were "special" friends, and that was enough for everyone to speculate.

At first, I didn't understand what they were doing at school. I asked his sister and got the weirdest response ever.

"Mila, we're here to get you married to my brother." For a moment, I was stunned at her words. I had not expected her to just show up at my workplace expect me to just marry her brother. Apparently, she had it all figured out.

She said if I accepted her proposal and married Pol that day, I would receive a monthly check from the Navy for housing allowance. It was a benefit that all married members of the Navy were entitled to. If I became his wife, then I would begin receiving the money on his behalf. I would be able to save for our big wedding.

She pitched this idea to me quite happily. My colleagues who caught up with some of our conversations were congratulating me as they walked by me. I could hear some of the girls, my students, giggling in the distance, and I stood there horrified. I didn't want to get married so quickly to him and for what, a benefit?

She waited for me outside the front of the school in their car. After her explanation, she had expected me to be as excited as she was. She hadn't seen anything in my eyes except for fear.

I was so scared of everything that was happening. I did what I thought was right and did it impulsively. I left my students to be watched by my co-teacher next door. I went to the back door of the school and escaped. I told my mom why I was home. Thankfully, my mother felt the same way, and she didn't let me go back to school after that.

She felt as did I that they would certainly make a second attempt to try and reach me at the school. And I agreed with her. I wasn't trying to ditch getting married when I ran away from the school. I always knew my parents would want me to settle down sooner or later, no matter how I insisted I wanted to stay a nun. So, that was something I had prepared myself for quite some time ago. However, I ran away because she had just appeared at my school out of nowhere. It was like they owned me, and they had a right to just walk into my life whenever they felt like it.

I understood their concerns about their son. Of course, he was young, and he was in the Navy. They wanted to see him married before he left for his posting in California, but trying to trick me into it wasn't very kind of them, and if I thought their first attempt was insane, I should have waited for the second one because the second one made my life very difficult in my town.

His family came to see my parents with a big box. Inside the box was a new gown, a new pair of shoes, and gloves, and a wig. They asked my parents if I can be invited to a party in town. There was no special occasion. It was just a gathering they were having, and they needed me around. My parents had no idea what it was all about.

They mentioned that it was a dance. They thought it would be fun if Pol and I attended it. I thought it was a terrible idea because I didn't know how to dance.

I knew everyone in town was attending this event. I didn't want to make a fool of myself in front of the whole town. I was unwilling to go, but my parents accepted the invitation. The only condition they put was that my grandma and cousins would escort me to the party.

They came to pick me up in their car right on time. I felt and looked like a Disney princess. We drove to the party to find it packed with people. There was a big crowd. Not all the people there were guests. Many of them were spectators who just wanted to enjoy the guests and their dances.

Chairs were lined up, and the stage was set with a band. This was my first ever date in life. I had never dated before, and I had never been kissed before. This was the first time in my life where I had been in public and on a date. I was so scared and embarrassed that I sat all through the party. Pol asked me a couple of times for a dance, but I kept turning him down. After an hour or so, when you noticed all the other couples enjoying themselves, I realized perhaps dancing wasn't so difficult.

The next time he asked me, I said yes. I stood up nervously. We started dancing slowly in the corner of the stage. I stepped on his feet a couple of times. He remained a gentleman. In the next few minutes, he had taken control of my body. He was slowly swaying us in the middle of the stage, and I was dancing along with him.

In the next few minutes, I had forgotten well about not being able to dance. He had taken us in the middle of the stage.

When we got to the middle of the dancing floor, the band stopped, and everybody went back to their seats except us. The toastmaster announced our names and requested that if we could dance one more time. Apparently, the two of us were the star couple of the night. I had no time to reject because I was in his arms. Everybody applauded for us in support.

We danced again and quite gracefully. It was a beautiful experience and one of the best nights of my life. I had lived a fantasy with him, and I had enjoyed every moment of it.

What happened after the party was anything but enjoyable. As the night ended, I went back home happily. The next day, I heard rumors that snatched all of my glee. The whole town was buzzing with the news that I was pregnant!

3

"Do not ask me to abandon or forsake you! For wherever you go, I will go, wherever you lodge I will lodge, your people shall be my people, and your God my God. Wherever you die, I will die, and there be buried. May the Lord do so and so to me, and more besides, if aight but death separates me from you! "

Ruth 1:16-17

The Wedding I Didn't Expect!

The party I was invited to ended up being a blast. I danced my heart away, and all of us went home satisfied and tired all at the same time. In my sleepy state, I barely had time to talk about the events at the party. I just changed and fell asleep, hoping to wake up to an even brighter morning than the party I had yesterday.

However, the morning brought some strange news. As soon as I was out and about, I learned that everyone in town was gossiping about me. 'Someone' had spread a rumor that I was pregnant. And after I became aware of it, I knew who was behind it. The night before was nothing but a trick by Pol's family. They had taken me to the party, made our relationship public, and then spread rumors of my pregnancy. They thought that after all of this, my parents would feel pressured by society, and instead of believing me, they would force me to marry him.

Thankfully, my parents knew me better than anyone. When I tried to explain myself to them, they believed me immediately. They knew I was more interested in my service to the Church. So, they understood I would never lose my virginity. They didn't believe a word of the defamation they were trying to create for me.

I was able to slip out of a tight corner once again. But this time, I had my doubts about what kind of a relationship I was a part of. Did he really care about me? If he did, he wouldn't have spread rumors that would damage my reputation in society. I wasn't exactly looking forward to our marriage after all this. These tricks they were playing had ruined my mood completely, and I couldn't trust them at all. I was so angry. All my friends knew, and they told me about it. I was embarrassed. I was afraid of what people will say about me. I was so fed up with these tricks. Now, I was literally counting the days left until he would finally leave.

I felt so miserable after all this that I wanted to let go of this relationship once and for all. I wanted to end it all, but I knew there was still some time for him to leave for the US. I knew they would try to reach out to me again. And they did.

The night after the party, his relatives came to my place. His mom and some of his other relatives were in this group. The first thing they did was pretty much out of etiquette. They showed up at our place without prior notice. We were in complete shock when they all barged in, carrying a lot of food with them. They were acknowledging we couldn't have been prepared because they arrived suddenly.

They had come over to discuss our proposal and insisted they wouldn't leave without getting a date for marriage. Their arrival made things more complicated for me than before. My parents thought I had known about their arrival since before and I hadn't mentioned it to them. They felt I had decided to get married without their consent, which wasn't true at all.

I told them that I had no knowledge of what they were talking about. Pol's relatives thought they had wasted their time due to some confusion and finally left when I didn't give in to their baseless claims.

They thought they wasted their time, so everybody went home. They were all very disappointed, but I couldn't care less. It was my life at stake. I didn't want to put it on the line for a bunch of people who only remembered us at weddings and funerals.

Pol asked his family and this time invited my relatives to visit us one more time, and they did because of him. On the second day, they negotiated with my parents, but nothing happened. Then they came back the third, and as they say, the third time's the charm. This time, my parents agreed as well, and they had finally concocted a marriage plan.

Pol's mother was the spokeswoman of the night. She explained to my parents that Pol had only a few days left and he had soon to report to America. She explained to everybody that I would be able to secure a good future if I married their son in place of marrying a local boy in town because he was in the US navy.

My father didn't hesitate when he answered in response in front of everybody that wealth was of little matter before my happiness. My father had his own concerns about this proposal, and he didn't think twice before speaking up about them. He was my guardian, and he had every right to protect me. He said, "How can I trust your son will be faithful to our daughter? Navy has a girl at every port who would stay around him while he was away from home. He can betray my daughter any time he wants."

My father also mentioned that as Pol had come from a broken family, he couldn't trust him to abide by our vows forever. His father had left his mother for another woman when Pol was only one year old.

Everything that was happening very fast-paced and absurd, and then something completely unexpected happened. Pol went to my dad and knelt in front of him. He told him this was not going to happen to us, and he will love me and adore me forever.

I wish I could go back in time and hold him to his words because now I know they were just words. He had never actually meant any of that. He had made sure that our marriage was not the beautiful dream I had created, and he broke it every time I tried to turn it into one.

At the time, however, Pol's tricks worked, and my parents finally agreed to the wedding. The Church had a regulation to keep the marriage for 28 days before he left. But as he didn't have enough time, we kept it for 26 days only and mentioned the incorrect number of days on the certificate.

Going into this wedding, I was a skeptic and didn't know what to expect. But then I received an unexpectedly beautiful wedding. The sponsors were all hand-picked by my sister-in-law. The secretary of defense, doctors, lawyers, and some wealthy couples in our country all attended our wedding. One of my sisters-in-law had a connection to the government in our country, and she was friends with lots of wealthy people and military officers. All of them added a different flavor to our ceremony.

I fell back into the endless abyss of love as we were finally married and together. I was finally looking forward to the honeymoon, one that was going to be just as eventful as the wedding!

4

Let me hear sounds of joy and gladness;

Let the bones you crushed rejoice. Psalm 51:10

Marriage - Not for the Weak-Hearted

I began my married life happily. Our wedding was great, and I was experiencing all sorts of new things. I had never been kissed before. But a couple of days before our wedding, Pol caught me on the way to the bathroom and kissed me. No one was around at the time.

This new stage in the journey of my life should have been the best, but I came across things I had never seen before. My wedding night wasn't so pleasant.

No one else knew the reason for it, but I spent my wedding night crying. Pol had missed the rehearsal dinner to visit his ex-girlfriend with my brother-in-law. So, that was unexpected, and yet it was my life now. I had to learn to live things, even if I wasn't okay with them.

The reception was in our home. Our home was nicely decorated, even our backyard. They had hired a lively band. It was an elegant wedding. They had professionally decorated our house and Church.

I knew things weren't that great for the wedding between Pol and me, but I was hoping the honeymoon would change that. On our honeymoon, however, I had to face another challenge. His family accompanied us on the honeymoon as if we were going on a vacation or something. They wouldn't let us enjoy any private moment with each other.

I learned later that a few of Pol's siblings didn't want him to get married. Especially Crispy who invited all the important people of the town.

Nothing like this had ever happened in my family. I was the younger of two siblings in my home. There is a seven-year age-gap between my sister and me, and she wasn't jealous of me.

I had to bear with my in-laws for six months until my visa and other naval requirements were completed. My sisters-in-law were quite mean to me. I used to cry at night and regretted ever agreeing to this marriage, but then I couldn't go back on my decision. I never told my parents about any of this. I didn't want them to worry.

Soon, my visa arrived, and I had to say goodbye to my family. It was a sad time. And yet, there was hope that I would have a great beginning with my husband.

After six months, he came back. A cargo plane flew us to the US from the Clark Air Base. When we arrived in Monterey, CA, we lived in a one-bedroom duplex apartment close to the Naval Post Graduate School base.

When we finally arrived in Monterey, California, where he was posted, it was like we had stepped into a new world, and we had to look forward to a new life.

We didn't have a car, so we walked to work, the Church, groceries, everywhere. I stayed most of the time at home. I tried my best to learn everything I should know to become a good dedicated wife. Pol liked that for me to be home all the time. But, on the contrary, I wanted to continue teaching in the US.

I had started my new life positively, but Pol had another plan. He made things so difficult for me. I had been teaching in my home town. When we settled in California, I wanted to teach here too. But he just wouldn't let me. We disagreed on so many things. He just wanted me to stay at home and be a housewife.

I waited for his approval for quite some time, but then I just couldn't take it any longer. I was frustrated. I had never stayed home for such a long time.

While he was at work, one day, I called a taxi, and I went to Monterey Unified School District and inquired how to get a teaching job. I was told I had to take the National Teacher test. I asked the date, place, and time and intended to do it. I forgot that Pol didn't know where I went so I hurried back home because he didn't know I had left home.

Well, he was not home from work yet when I arrived. After two weeks, I received a notice from the School Board that came in the mail about the exam. I went to take the test, and I passed it. I was then given the certification that I could teach in Monterey, California. I was so happy that I could teach, but we argued for a while because he didn't want me to leave the house. He wanted me to be a homemaker, but later I convinced him to let me teach.

Pol was very angry with this whole situation. He didn't want me to continue my education or stay in the new job. However, contrary to his wishes, I stayed in the job.

This time we loaned a car, so I could go to work. I was given a job at Del Rey Woods Elementary School but not the job I wanted. Because of my heavy accent, the children couldn't understand me, so the school placed me to be a school librarian. This job gave me more opportunity to communicate a lot more with the students, to improve my English and diction.

I treasured that experience beyond anything. It was a learning curve, and I gladly took it on. My parents had always taught me that education was the key to a successful life, and I had a habit of taking their advice to heart. They were always right about everything.

After six months, I became an Instructional specialist. They hired a speech teacher, and I was trained to speak better. I was so lucky to be given that attention at the school. Everybody was so nice. This school trained me from scratch. They showed me the way to become a better teacher. They included me in all the activities at school to make me feel at home.

After a year, when I got better at English, I became a full-time teacher teaching Kindergarten. But then I was just finishing with my teaching contract as a full-time teacher that year, and Pol received a letter from the Navy that he was ready to get transferred to Norfolk, Virginia for three years' deployment at sea. Normally, ships will go to sea for ten days to two weeks each month for training operations in preparation for deployment. Extended operations away from the home port can be up to six to nine months, and ships are typically deployed once every eighteen to twenty-four months.

This is where the tension started in our relationship. I didn't want to leave my first teaching job in the US. So, I told him that I was not going with him to Norfolk, Virginia. What he did then, he didn't re-enlist in the US Navy. He didn't want to leave me in Monterey by myself. So, he had no choice but to look for a job in Monterey and in the neighboring county. He applied everywhere, but unfortunately he couldn't get a job anywhere.

After a year, we had to make a quick decision of whether or not he will be re-enlisting because his dad and my grandma both passed in the same year, and he wanted to go home, but we couldn't afford the plane tickets. Only the Navy plane could take us back home.

So I resigned from my job immediately, he re-enlisted in the Navy, and we went back home. After a month of our stay home, we flew back to the US by the Navy plane straight to Norfolk, Virginia, where he had to report on his new assignment, a three years' deployment at sea. We had only one car. I dropped him off before going to work.

Looking back at our short stay in Monterey, California, it was a great beginning! I made friends with the faculty and administrators at the school in Monterey. I made friends with our neighbors too, at Church and everywhere. I didn't have problems making friends everywhere I went. In reality, I had co-teachers at Del Rey Woods School in Monterey who visited us one day in our place and tried to convince me to buy their house at 17 Miles Drive in Monterey. They said they would be resigning as teachers as they wanted to become nuns, and they chose me to make me the new owner of their house.

It's a beautiful house by the water. At the time, I didn't know about Real Estate investment, and that house was only sold to me at $65,000. My co-teacher and the owner said that all I needed at the time was $500 to put as a down payment to buy the house. I think it was a privilege being in the Navy. I was still not convinced to buy it. After fifteen years, when I went to visit Monterey, I found out the place was sold to the third owner for $5,000,000—We lost a huge opportunity.

We faced good times and bad times living in Monterey, but we enjoyed a great beginning. The only problem I remember was when I encountered a weird lady who came to visit our place. She was skinny, pretty, and tall. She was a good match with my husband's height. I didn't remember her as a friend but an acquaintance. I thought I saw her at church every Sunday; she sat in the pew in front of the place where we used to sit. As a routine before the mass, we introduced each other inside the Church, shook hands before the mass.

I noticed, she always reached out to shake my husband's hands before mine. I ignored her as I didn't know her well and would only see her at Church. But one day, when I came home sick from work, I found her in our living room having coffee with my husband. I heard them laughing and giggling as I walked in through our front door. When I entered, I looked at them, but I could not talk much because I wasn't well. When I lay on the bed, I heard her saying goodbye to my husband, and I heard the door close.

When I asked my husband later about why she was at our house, he said she was just stopping by to say hello to both of us. I thought it was justified, so I didn't make a big deal out of it, but it didn't sound right. After that incident, I didn't see her anymore, and we didn't have enough time anyway to know her well because we were about to leave Monterey. My husband's two years' duty station was over.

The night of the wedding rehearsal, when he went to see his previous girlfriend, and the unpredictable appearance of this lady at my house with Pol in the living room was a confusing beginning, and that question lingered in my mind—nudging our problems and my doubts slowly to the forefront.

When I embraced family life, I was eager to have children. It could have been that Pol was always out for deployment, or God planned for us not to have children too soon. I took fertility pills and tried all the possible ways to conceive easily but was not successful. Pol said, if we got to our 10th year wedding anniversary and we still didn't have a baby, we would adopt one girl.

I started offering fervent prayers to Saint Gerard Majella, the patron saint for children and unexpected pregnancy. It worked as I got pregnant soon after. Our first baby was born eleven days after our 9th anniversary. One day, when I was at work, I felt so sick. I went to see a Navy doctor.

They ran a pregnancy test, and the test said it was negative. I was assuming I would be better from my sickness the following day, but I got sicker. So, I went to see a private practice doctor. He also ran a pregnancy test, and it turned positive this time. That was when I finally announced my pregnancy. Could you believe that I felt miserable while carrying the baby for nine months because of the confusion caused by the contradicting results? I was scared that this was a false pregnancy, which they said was a possibility. Every day, I made sure that I could feel the baby in my womb. There were nights praying and crying. I asked God to make it a real baby—terrible feelings!! However, my first baby was healthy and was born on Mother's Day.

The doctor called him a "miracle" baby; I thought this was the only baby we would have. However, I never stopped hoping, I never stop praying to Saint Gerard Majella, and I asked for another child. After three years, I gave birth to another beautiful miracle baby boy. My prayers had been answered. Everything is possible for God if you believe and ask with a pure heart. In my marriage, there were a lot of issues. Starting from the very beginning, he had not spared the rehearsal dinner. I wanted to know why my brother in law drove Pol to his ex-girlfriend on the night before my wedding day? Why was my husband unable to attend the dress rehearsal? Why did his family members allow this to happen, knowing that it was our wedding the next day?

Crispy, my sister-in-law, wrote letters to Pol while he was on deployment at sea and told lies that I was mistreating her and my mother-in-law and drove them out of my house. It was their choice to move out to another relative's residence because I worked all day and had no time to serve them, cook, do their laundry, among other things. Their expectation from me was that I would be there to serve them. However, that wasn't possible while I was working and attending to my children's needs as well.

One day, she called me and told me that I was not suitable to be his brother's wife. She said that her doctor friend, who was more beautiful than me, would be a better match and that I snatched him away from that relationship.

I didn't know that Pol had a relationship with her doctor friend.

When they lived with us, every time Crispy passed by me, she called me names. She knew Pol was at the deployment and will not know the torture. She treated me nice when Pol was around and made me miserable when he was out at sea.

All of these issues made one thing clear; marriage is not for the weak-hearted!

5

For your name's sake, Lord, give me life; in your

justice,

lead me out of distress.

Psalm 143: 11

Fissures and Fractures

During this time, Pol had completed his duty at sea, and his next assignment required him to perform his shore-duty at the Naval Amphibious Base in Norfolk, Virginia. I was gullible enough to believe that Pol's new assignment would be helpful for our family in one way or the other. I thought that, after his return, he would not only share the household responsibilities with me but that he would also perform his obligations as a husband.

Unfortunately for me, that was not the case. In fact, now that I reflect back on my life, I have come to realize that his new assignment actually drove us even further apart. Rather than help me maintain the household and perform his fatherly duties, it felt as if

I had to take care of Pol the same way I was supposed to look after my sons. Due to the added responsibility of Pol, my schedule became tougher, and I was unable to keep up with it. What truly hurt me was the fact that...

...Pol never seemed to do anything that I expected from him. It felt like I was being forced to experience a series of disappointments, and I could not escape. Nonetheless, I knew that I had no alternative, and, as such, I put my blood, sweat, and tears into managing my job and my maternal and wifely duties.

For a short time, things were going as well as they could have. However, one day I found out that Pol was cheating on me with a WAVE – a Navy woman who was also the daughter of a Captain in the Navy. I was heartbroken and angry. I knew that he was not the best person, but I had never thought that he would betray me this way. After giving the matter some thought, I reported his illegitimate relationship with the WAVE to his higher-ups. Since the girl's father was a well-respected officer in the Navy, both he and the WAVE were disciplined. I also confronted him regarding his unfaithful behavior, but our conversation was not fruitful at all. I felt as if he was repeatedly trying to gaslight me into thinking that I was the one who had driven him to commence a relationship with the girl.

Regardless, I was pretty much content with the way I had dealt with the situation, and I strongly believed that getting reprimanded by his higher-ups in the

Navy would have taught Pol a much-needed lesson. I also thought that he would not be unfaithful to me again, but alas, I was wrong.

Besides teaching at the school, I was also searching for a part-time job that could ease our financial needs. It just came to happen that both Pol and I were recruited to provide cleaning-service to the Navy. My responsibilities included cleaning the building, mopping the bathroom floors, taking care of the trash, etc. Again, things between Pol and I seemed to be going as smoothly as they could have until one day, he sexually assaulted another WAVE. The WAVE was on duty that night, and she reported to the Navy that Pol had made an unwelcome move on her. Things were taken to court, and I was called up to testify regarding

Pol's behavior. The judge asked me if Pol was a good husband and a good man, and, due to my faithfulness, I naïvely spoke in his favor. At the time, I truly could not convince myself that Pol was an evil man. As it turned out, my words ended up being the deciding factor in the judge's decision, and Pol was not demoted from his rank.

Before Pol finally retired from the Navy, God had been kind enough to bless us with two adorable sons. At that point, my eldest son was eight years old, and his younger brother was just five. Both my children needed a strong father figure in their lives that they could look up to. They required a role-model who could not only be a mentor for them but someone who could also resolve their innumerable queries about life.

As such, I thought that Pol's retirement would be very productive for us. It would allow both of my sons to spend more time with him and, as a consequence, develop an unbreakable bond with their father. These thoughts also made me happy, and I came to believe that retirement would change Pol for the better. But as I came to find out, I had been day-dreaming, and those dreams were short-lived.

When he finally did retire, he and I managed to buy a restaurant with the money we had saved up so far. Pol made me know that he would be responsible for managing the various operations of the restaurant. Apart from continuing my job as a teacher, I had also become involved in real estate and was responsible for looking after our properties. Pol and I also owned a motel near our restaurant, and I was on good terms with the neighbors. My neighbors were caring, and they always looked after me.

After some time had elapsed, my neighbors informed me that Pol had been bringing women to the motel. At first, I did not believe it, but I slowly came to my senses. After retirement, Pol was no longer fearful of being reprimanded the way he had been because he thought that I would always rescue him in any given circumstance. Consequently, his unfaithful habits had resurfaced. When I confronted him and informed him about what our neighbors had told me, he denied everything. He manipulated me into believing that I was a distrustful and suspicious wife and that I was driving him crazy. He deflected anything that I said by attacking my character and personality, and it seemed like we were constantly fighting about women.

After this instance, my relationship with Pol devolved quickly. Moreover, I came to realize that even though I was making a good sum of money, I was unable to tend to my children. I felt that I was slacking when it came to my maternal responsibilities. Even though Pol was responsible for managing the various operations that went on in the restaurant, I was the one who had to constantly make sure that the restaurant's hygiene was maintained in case there was a surprise visit from the health inspector. The feeling that I was not a good mother gradually amplified. What made things even worse was the fact that I was unable to take my children to church, and this internally destroyed me. The reason I couldn't was that our restaurant was extremely busy on Sundays, and people from all around the vicinity came to enjoy breakfast at our eatery.

At this point in time, I knew that I needed to close the restaurant. Money did not matter as long as I was keeping good care of my children. My sons have always been my first priority in life, and I realized that they were getting older. I needed to dedicate as much time as I could to take care of them before they left my home in pursuit of their various ambitions and dreams.

However, my thoughts were constantly plagued by the devil, who kept reminding me that I would be giving up all the luxuries that I possessed in life. He reminded me that if I closed the restaurant, I would not be able to afford the expensive private education that my children were getting. He kept reminding me of when I had gone to a casino with my husband on a trip to Atlantic City in New Jersey. Our family had been living a wealthy life, and that was reflected in the fact that I had a maid who cleaned up my house and a gardener to look after our yard.

Moreover, my family and I were always going on vacation during Christmas and Thanksgiving. The devil constantly reminded me of all these things, and I had to honestly ask myself if I was willing to give up every luxury that I had accumulated in my life. If there are some things that I can say about myself with utmost certainty, they are that I never gamble or drink, but I love shopping.

In my desperation and confusion, I cried to God, and I asked Him for guidance. I came to find out a few months later that the city had bought out the entire area where my restaurant had been located. Apparently, there had been a shortage of urban residences, and, as such, the city had decided to build new homes in their newly bought land. I thanked God for answering my prayers, and I could not believe how lucky I had been. At that moment, I was just so happy that I did not have to choose between my children and their future, as selling the restaurant would have meant giving up the private education my children had so far been receiving.

Now that the restaurant was gone, I transferred them to another school division that was closer to my home. My decision to do so was prompted by the desire to be there for my children when they returned from their school. I also decided to complete my master's degree in education. However, I knew that doing so was going to be difficult as I would have to manage both my teaching job as well as the apartments we owned.

Since the income from the restaurant had ended, I thought that completing my master's degree in education would help me get a better job that would compensate for the loss of income from the restaurant. I firmly believe that this was the toughest time of my life. There were nights I stayed up to work on my thesis with my feet soaking in hot water as they were sore from working all day.

At that time, I knew that there was no sleep or rest for me because I had to perform my responsibilities as a teacher the very next day. Pol also started looking for jobs, but he was unable to find one. I thought that he was doing so to help me, but I was wrong. When he finally did start a business in which he sold used cars, he made a good income but did not contribute enough to sustain the expenses of the household and for the children's education. Things became so bad that I had to sell the apartments we owned.

I kept praying to God, begging the Lord to give me more strength for the sake of my children. I felt as if my life was a roller-coaster. Whenever I moved on from an incident, my life would make another frightening shift, manipulating me into thinking that it would be the last one.

After coming home one day, my husband demanded $10,000, saying that he needed the money for his business. He told me that the profit he had made yesterday fell out of his pocket that had a hole in it. I did see the hole in his pocket, but I could not help but wonder why Pol did not see it in the first place before keeping his money in there. I was always a nervous wreck because whenever Pol demanded something from me, and I refused to please him, he would follow me to my work and embarrass me in front of my co-workers and students.

Whenever I make decisions, I always think about my children's welfare first and foremost. So, when my bank officer advised me to put Pol in jail, my internal voice nagged me not to do so as it would radically affect my children's lives. Apparently, Pol had loaned $17,000 from the Navy Federal Credit Union and used my car as collateral. When he did not pay back the loan, the bank sent me a letter.

I was shocked, not knowing what he had done. I was told by the bank that my credit will be ruined if I didn't pay back Pol's loan. As such, I was forced to settle with the NFU by paying them $12,000. Later, the NFU told me that I could not deliver on Pol's behalf, and Pol must be the one to settle the remaining amount as he was a co-owner. For a while, I suffered since I could not charge anything on my credit cards.

I thought that everything would be alright, but I was wrong. After some time, I received another letter regarding outstanding POA dues at the Middle Plantation Association. I was dismayed. I went to their office and found out that Pol had forged my son's signatures.

I had no idea how all of this came about because my eldest son was only 16 years old, and Michael was just 13. My name was signed as a guarantor. I could not believe that Pol would go to such extreme lengths for money. The fact that he forged the signature of his teenage son goes on to reflect the kind of abysmal father he was.

Despite all these tribulations, I kept my children unaware of what was happening. I didn't want them to be involved. They were too young to understand, and it would not have been a good idea to distract their young minds from their studies and co-curricular activities. I thought of seeking counseling or talking to friends about my problems, but I could not find time due to my busy schedule, so I just kept praying to God.

When things got really rough to handle alone, I used to call my late parents and my late grandma for help. Even when I was pregnant with my eldest son, Paul, I told my parents that I would need their help when the baby was finally born. I had been incredibly occupied with my teaching responsibilities, and I could not make proper preparations for the baby. As such, I had reached out to my parents for help. I consider myself extremely lucky when it comes to my parents.

Upon my request, my mother and father had immediately made their way over to Virginia, where they did more than just help me in looking after my kids. Just having them there had a positive impact on my personality, and I had begun to feel more confident in the regular dealings of my life, knowing that I could resort to my parents for any sort of assistance or guidance.

The fact that they were there to support me helped me immensely, and I felt that things were going how they were supposed to for once. Unfortunately, I was under the delusion that my parents would always be there for me. A few years later, my mind was diverted from my marriage problems to something much worse. I came to find out that my father had fallen gravely ill, and he soon passed away. I was next to him in his final moments, and I could not control my tears when my father drew his last breath. His death was not only a shocker for me, but it also sent my mother into a frenzy of sorts.

She became extremely depressed, and she could not take care of herself as she was in a wheelchair for a year. I knew my mother needed me the same way I had needed her when I was a kid, and, as such, I cut down on some of my work. I started attending to her needs. However, she kept getting sicker until she passed away seven years later. Within a decade, I had lost both of my parents, and I felt completely lost. I had thought that I would not be able to get through that phase of my life. The death of my mother had prompted me down a road of sadness, depression, and various other feelings that I cannot even begin to describe. I just know that none of them were happy.

Even while writing this, I cannot help but tear up. After all, she had been my mother, and I never imagined that I would lose her this way. But that is the sad reality of life.

It hits you the hardest when you least expect it. Moreover, both Michael and Paul were just teenagers at the time when my parents passed away. They were both so close to their grandparents, and it hurt me even more, knowing that they had lost someone so dear to them. To this day, I mourn for my parents' death, and I know that my sons do too. My mind races back to the memories that I shared with them whenever I think about them or come across one of their pictures.

At that moment, I smile because I thank God for blessing me with such amazing parents. I also feel extremely lucky because I was able to spend so many wonderful times with my parents, and thinking about those times makes me extremely happy.

However, at the same time, I feel a certain hollowness in my heart. It seems that something that was supposed to be there has gone missing, and I can never find it again, no matter how hard I search for it.

Sometimes, I feel as I am being swallowed whole by this emptiness, and, often, I feel as I am suspended mid-air in the fetal position. I miss my parents terribly, and I hope that they are in a better place. In fact, knowing their kind nature, I know for a fact that they are in heaven looking down upon me. I know that they must be proud of me for how far I have come in my life, and they would be praying for me.

At that time, I was also aware that I could not let my sadness overcome me as my sons were getting bigger, and they needed me more than ever. As such, I knew that my parents would not want me to grieve and that they would have prompted me to overcome my depression and take care of my beautiful boys. Despite knowing all of this, it was still quite hard for me to find the willpower I needed to start taking care of myself and my family again. Nonetheless, I stood up once again by finding inspiration in something that my grandma frequently told me. She always advised me to be courageous and to be religious, and, acting upon her advice, I once again started fulfilling my manifold responsibilities.

6

"I cried to you, Lord, because of my afflictions. And

He answered me Out of the belly of Sheol I cried,

And You heard my voice." Jonah 2:2

Grief and Drugs

Soon after my parents' death, I had to muster up the strength to turn my attention and energy towards my two sons. Of course, it was very difficult for me to bear the emotional burden that came with losing my wonderful support system. However, I had no choice but to give my two sons the support they needed. They were getting older, and I wanted to be there for them—someone they could turn to whenever they wanted, someone they could share with whatever they hoped to discuss; I wanted to be their go-to person.

Unfortunately, my ex-husband, Pol, couldn't be there for them; he couldn't be the emotionally present father and support system for my children. He was too busy involved with the vulgarities of life, wasting away his precious time and money on gambling, drinking, and dating other women. It was late 1999 or early 2000s, I don't quite remember (the exact dates are blurred out), but my son Michael had just been promoted to Junior Year at Norfolk Academy in Norfolk, Virginia.

One day, before he left for school, Michael informed me that he felt a bit feverish. I wasn't quite alarmed, and I assumed it was probably the viral fever going around and didn't feel the need to ask him to stay back. However, Michael's condition worsened during his classes, and so he excused himself and returned home to rest. Pol, who didn't bother going to work that day, was oblivious to the idea that his son had a fever and had returned early from school that day.

While Michael was resting in his room, he overheard his father talking to a woman on the phone. It sounded like they had scheduled a date and were planning to meet that very evening. Naturally, Michael was alarmed; no kid wants to see their father cheating on their mother. He managed to get off of his bed and walk up to Pol, confronting him about his alleged affair.

Michael was straightforward; he expressed his concerns, sharing how distraught he was. He told him he could not believe that his own father was cheating on me, his wife, with a completely random woman. He shared his disappointments bluntly as no son wants to see their father break their mother's heart. However, my innocent son had no idea that this wasn't a new affair. He was oblivious to the idea that Pol, his father, would regularly sleep with other women.

When I returned from work that evening, my maternal instincts noticed how agitated my son was. Being the supportive mother I had planned to become, I approached him and lovingly questioned him about why he seemed so bothered, thinking maybe it was a fight with his friends or girl problems at school.

Initially, Michael held back; he probably didn't want to disappoint me, assuming I had no idea about Pol's regular affairs. He got up and entered the kitchen to grab a glass of water. Naturally, being a mother, I was used to pestering my children until I knew what was bothering them. I couldn't see them so disturbed and wanted to offer whatever I could to make them feel better. I followed Michael into the kitchen, held his hand, and looked straight into his concerned eyes, which tried to avoid eye contact as if he was hiding something from me.

Michael, my strong son, was so shaken up that I could see his watery eyes on the verge of crying. The poor boy couldn't hold back and illustrated the events that had unfolded in front of his eyes that afternoon. As a mother, I have always placed my sons' needs before my own, even emotionally. I couldn't dare see them go through such emotional turmoil. I didn't want him to know that I was already aware of Pol's questionable behavior, and so I decided to pretend as if I did not know anything from before. I pulled Michael into my warm embrace, patting his back, letting him know I was there for him. Despite knowing the truth, I mustered up the strength to lie to my son. I tried to present an alternative picture for him, letting him know that maybe the woman his father was talking to was probably one of his clients who had scheduled a meeting to buy a car that evening.

I was quite emotionally distraught as I said this and held my tears back, especially because Pol had brought his mess into the doors of my home and so close to my sons. I was quite infuriated, but I couldn't show that on my face. I had to pretend and put an act for my son because I didn't want his world to come crashing down with my own. Thankfully, my words did the trick; Michael seemed to have been convinced as he seemed quite comforted. However, I was certain that he would keep recalling the incident, keep thinking about all the possibilities that one phone call could've been.

A month or so following the incident, Michael, on returning from school one afternoon, rushed into his bedroom, locking the door shut behind him. Usually, upon his arrival, Michael would rush into my warm embrace, greeting me lovingly and sharing all the happenings and shenanigans of his day at school with me as we would both reflect on them together. However, that wasn't the case that afternoon.

Of course, I was quite alarmed, and I found his demeanor to be incredibly strange; nonetheless, I did not nag him, assuming his crush probably ended up with another guy. That night, around 11 pm, Michael finally got out of his bed and walked down towards me, requesting me to allow him to take a bath. I thought it was pretty late for Michael to be making such an odd request; however, I allowed him.

Considering his stranger behavior earlier that day, I figured he might have had an awful day at school, and the bath might be therapeutic for him. Michael slowly made his way towards the bathroom and opened the faucet to fill the bath-tub.

Around fifteen or so minutes later, I could still hear the water running down the faucet, which alarmed me further. I grew quite anxious, and my heart began to beat at the speed of light.

My maternal instincts told me that something was terribly wrong. I rushed towards the bathroom, leaving everything behind. I knocked and called out to

Michael, but he did not reply. I kept knocking until I saw the water running in from under the bathroom door. At that moment, I cannot articulate what I actually felt; my anxiety shot through the roof, and I suddenly felt the adrenaline pumping through my veins. I was shaking from within, but I had to control myself and be in my senses. He pushed the door open and went inside the room. I still tremble with fear whenever I think about what I saw that night.

My poor boy was lying motionless in the bath-tub; the water around him turned completely red as his right wrist was hanging over from the bath-tub. Michael had slit his wrists. I cannot explain in words the horror I went through that night. At that moment, my mind grew completely numb as I stood still staring at my son floating in the blood-red water. I don't know how and from where, but God gave me strength. I managed to snap out my horrific thoughts and rushed towards the phone to call the paramedics. I couldn't control my tears as they dripped down my face, I felt so helpless between the phone call, and until the ambulance arrived, I had no idea what to do. I didn't want to do anything that would make things worse than they already were. I just sat beside the bath-tub as I prayed to Jesus and hoped for the ambulance to arrive soon.

Thankfully, due to God's infinite grace, my son miraculously survived. The doctors informed me that had I been even a moment later, my son would not have lived to see another day. I cannot explain in words how grateful I am to Jesus for his love and support. It is because of God's countless blessings that my boy is still alive and well. It took a few weeks before Michael was discharged from the hospital. I couldn't imagine what emotional and psychological unrest my boy must have been going through that pulled him to take such a step.

A part of me kept questioning where it was that I went wrong. I kept recounting my steps, every incident, every moment from the past few weeks to remember if it was something that I did or do that pushed him towards these limits. On the doctor's suggestion, I also got Michael a psychiatrist. I wanted him to have the best care. The psychiatrist visited him regularly at the hospital to help him understand and find peace with himself.

Those few weeks of Michael in the hospital are probably one of the worst phases of my life. Before Michael attempted suicide, I had no indication that suggested that Michael was intoxicating himself with drugs or that he was hanging out with the wrong sort of crowd.

The only thing that seemed off about him was that he hadn't performed as well as he usually would in his last assessments. Perhaps, I should have paid more attention. I should've been more emotionally present. But, at the time, I assumed that it was perfectly natural for him to struggle with his academics as he had chosen really demanding subjects in his junior year. I had no idea there could have been other reasons why his performance in class fell.

Being perfectly honest here, I had begun to feel that I was a terrible mother who could not even figure out or see that her own son was in so much emotional and psychological pain that he had been planning to kill himself. Even as I am writing this, I cannot hold back my tears; I cannot help but cry. I used to always think that I was a great mother who always put her sons before herself. But after that incident, I can't think of myself that way anymore. My sons, however, keep reassuring me that I am a great mother; they keep telling me not to doubt my maternal instincts.

Nonetheless, at the time, I felt that the regular fights I had with my ex-husband, Pol, had directly driven my son to such extreme measures. For days, I could neither eat nor sleep. I had dark circles under my eyes, and there came a time when I could no longer cry; it felt as if the tears inside my eyes had dried up completely.

Michael was an excellent student. He had been performing well in every class; not only would he excel at his academics, but he would also regularly participate in various extracurricular activities, and would quite frankly, perform well in those as well. Oftentimes, he would stay beyond regular school hours to attend club meetings and activities. I could never imagine my life without Michael and the nights that he spent at the hospital made me immensely tense.

My anxiety would keep reminding me of how I could've lost my son that night had God not pushed me to go check on him, and thinking about that sends shivers down my spine. Just like his brother, he was extremely affectionate and loving towards me. Both of my sons were good children. Neither of them ever gave me any problems; sure, they were mischievous at times but, then again, that is the way all young kids are.

Due to Michael's hard work and amazing grades, his teachers were extremely pleased with him. They were immensely proud of everything Michael had achieved during his time at school. I remember some of his teachers telling me that it would be an honor for them to recommend Michael to prestigious colleges; they further reassured me that Michael would easily get admission in an Ivy-League College due to the innumerable talents he had up his sleeve.

Looking back at that haunting night, after the paramedics had taken Michael to the hospital, the doctors told me that I should go home and take some rest. I insisted on staying, but they believed it would be best for me if I go home and try to put my mind on something else.

I agreed, hoping they would know better. I also thought this way I could go home and pray for Michael in peace and be there with him first thing the next day. But before any of that, when I arrived at my place, I immediately went into Michael's room and rummaged through his drawers to find any indication that could explain what pushed Michael to take such a dreadful step. Much to my surprise, instead of coming across a possible explanation of his actions, I ended up finding a handgun that was hidden under some clothes in one of his drawers. I screamed with utter shock at the sight of the pitch-black handgun. I gathered my thoughts and decided to take the handgun and dispose of it safely, fearing that Michael might make another attempt at his life.

During this time, I cannot explain how hard it was to keep my calm, to try and remain to be the supportive mother I thought I was considering I had begun to doubt every move that I had made as Michael's mother.

When Michael was finally discharged from the hospital, I caught him searching for his gun one evening. However, I did not say anything. I am sure he realized that I had found the handgun and had taken it away, but he too did not say anything to me. I looked straight into his eyes without saying a word, hoping that he would confess to me whatever had compelled him to have such suicidal tendencies. But he did not say anything, and I did not want to nag him any further.

After all, my sweet little baby boy had just returned from the hospital, and he was exhausted and weak from all those days in the hospital recovering. Both of us remained silent for a while before I finally wrapped my arms around him. My eyes swelled up, and I told him that I loved him more than anything else in this world. I reassured him he could come and talk to me whenever he wanted.

I wanted him to know I was there for him, and I cannot imagine living in a world without him. I could feel my shoulder dampen from his tears; just like me, he could not control his tears, and we cried in each other's warm embrace.

Before we moved apart, I told Michael that both he and his brother are an essential part of my life and that they give me the reason to live that their upbringing is my purpose in life. I told him that the only reason I manage to wake up every day in the morning is that I want to continue sharing this world with them. I could not muster up the courage to tell him that I had disposed of his handgun, and we never discussed anything about it from that point onwards.

Three weeks later, Michael came up to me and informed me that he wanted to move to California. Keeping in mind the events that had transpired the preceding month, I assumed that he must have been under a lot of pressure to make such an impulsive demand.

It was quite a brave decision to undertake. However, at the time, I thought maybe a fresh beginning could be quite helpful to bring Michael's life back on track. It's always great to start afresh and turn over a new leaf. A few of my cousins lived in California. I was really close with them to the point that I basically considered them my own sisters. I was sure that

Michael would be in good hands if he was to stay with them, and, as such, after much pondering over my own thoughts, I decided to allow Michael to move to California.

Before he embarked on this journey, I made proper arrangements with my cousins, who happily agreed to host Michael for however long he needed to stay there. Upon his arrival in California, my cousins enrolled Michael into a public school.

I was hopeful that California would assist Michael in recovering from his depression and hopefully help him forget the past few weeks that had been quite painful for him. Unfortunately, all my hopes and expectations were in vain. Two weeks after he had moved there, Michael had made some new friends at school who invited him to a birthday party that was supposed to take place after school. One of my cousins was supposed to drive him home after school had ended. However, Michael never arrived at the decided spot where my cousin was waiting for him to pick him from. Apparently, some of his friends had taken him to an abandoned building.

There they had pressured him into consuming alcohol, cigarettes, and ecstasy. Michael, who had never done anything like this before, no drugs whatsoever, got extraordinarily high and fainted. His friends, who probably panicked, left him unconscious in the desolate building all alone. My poor boy laid there on the cold, cemented floor of the empty building, unconscious, with no sign of help whatsoever around him.

7

"The Son of Man will be handed over to the chief of priests and the scribes, and they condemn him to death and hand him over to the Gentiles to be mocked and scourged and crucified," Matthew 20: 18-19

Therapy & Divorce

Naturally, when there was no sign of Michael at the designated spot, my cousin began to panic, more so because I had trusted her with the well-being of my son and his absence for quite some time made her worried sick. Thankfully, however, due to God's endless grace and watchful eye over my son, my cousin was able to locate Michael. She saw Michael sprawled face-down on the floor, unconscious, all alone with countless cigarette buds and empty bottles of alcohol lying next to his motionless body.

Despite my cousin's anxiety peaking, she was able to gather all her wits, and she immediately called 9-1-1 for an ambulance. The ambulance arrived shortly at the desolate building, and the paramedics carried

Michael to a nearby hospital. My cousin waited till the next day before she called me; I am glad she did so. I am sure she didn't want me to panic miles away from California.

She called me first thing in the morning and told me everything that had transpired the previous night. When I heard about what Michael went through only a few weeks after that unfortunate incident that I had still not fully recovered from, I began to feel dizzy. It was as if the walls around me were closing in on me, crushing me in between. I could not for the life of me comprehend what my cousin was saying.

When she told me that Michael had overdosed on drugs, I could not believe her. I could not believe that my innocent boy was capable of such a questionable act. It was just so unlike him. At the time, I blamed myself for everything that had occurred, first the suicide attempt and now this. I regretted my decision to allow Michael to move to California, especially at a time when he was so vulnerable.

I blamed myself for leaving him alone to fend for himself when he needed me the most. Michael had still not fully recovered from what had transpired a month or so ago. I should have known better, I thought. After the call ended, I immediately made my way towards the airport and booked an emergency flight to California.

Eight hours later, I had arrived at my cousin's place. The flight was awful, and I couldn't stop thinking about what my poor son must have been going through. On top of that, I kept blaming myself, and the claustrophobic setting of the airplane was only making me feel more suffocated. I cannot describe how I managed to pass through that approximately 8-hour-long travel time, but I somehow managed to reach my cousin's place.

The first thing I did was ask my cousin to drive me to the hospital to meet Michael. I wanted to see my son; I wanted him to know I was here for him. When I saw my Michael, my heart pierced. He looked so skinny, pale, and weak. It was a haunting sight, one I could never wish upon anyone, not even the worst of my enemies. I cannot gather the words to describe what he looked like; the most I can bring myself to say is that he seemed soulless.

I could tell the moment I saw my son lying helplessly in the hospital bed that after this experience, he would never be the same again. I remember standing next to his bed and bawling my eyes out as he could not recognize me, his own mother. It was like someone who had recently come out of a coma. Michael appeared delusional and had no idea where he was.

What hurt me most was that my baby boy was incredibly scared; he was trembling, and it felt like he could not make sense of whatever was going on around him. A few minutes later, he fainted again. By then, the doctor had realized that I was his mother, and he told me that it would take a miracle for Michael to survive. My body grew completely numb upon hearing the doctor's comment, and the floor swept away from beneath me.

It is difficult to describe what I was feeling, it was horrible, and no mother should ever go through what I did. My entire body was in terrible pain, but I felt hollow. I wanted to cry, but I could not as I knew it would not do anything; I wanted to do something more, but during all this time, I only continued to feel more helpless.

More than anything in this world, I wanted Michael back, alive and well. I no longer cared about what kind of man he would grow up to be if he was to survive. I just wanted him alive because, at that point, I realized that I would always love him no matter whatever happened. I realized that my world would never be the same if he left me that night. I continued praying to God, hoping for another miracle. I knew He was there for him before, and I wanted Him to be there for him again.

I could not blame anyone for what had happened to Michael. My cousin felt very guilty about the events that had transpired as she believed she was at fault considering I had trusted her with Michael, but I reassured her that she did whatever she could to save my boy's life. I tried to comfort myself by thinking that this must have happened for a reason, God is the best of all planners, and He does what is always best for the rest of us. I kept reminding myself that. What I was going through was one of the most painful feelings I have ever experienced in my life.

Seeing my son rise to the top of the world after recovering from that traumatic experience just to watch him topple down to the ground once again caused me a great deal of grief and hurt. In such turbulent times, the only thing that kept me going was my mother's words: "Be courageous and be religious." I kept praying to God to give my son another chance, and I knew if there was anyone who could help him, it was Him. I remained hopeful for a better future for Michael.

Nonetheless, staying optimistic was not an easy task. For days, I could not bring myself to eat or sleep. I felt lost and alone. Desolation, fear, guilt, anger, sadness, and disappointment are just a few of the feelings that remained tied around my neck and choked me. Perhaps, it is futile to describe whatever I was feeling; none of the feelings that I am aware of come close to describing my emotional state at that time.

Perhaps, what made matters worse was that I felt like all of my dreams for Michael had disappeared, all those hopes of seeing him become a doctor, marry the love of his life, become a father, etc.

I began to cry as I thought of the future I had hoped for him; I couldn't imagine not being able to see my hopes come to fruition. A few days later, the doctor finally informed me that Michael's condition had gotten better, enough for him to be able to go home. I politely requested the kind doctor to give Michael a muscle relaxant as I planned on taking him to Virginia directly. I cannot recall where Pol, his father, was at that time; it goes on to show what kind of a despicable father he was. He didn't care one bit about his sons, let alone me. Regardless, Michael and I arrived back at our home in Virginia the very next day. Back home, my foremost priority was to make sure that Michael's emotional state got better.

I took him to various therapists and counselors day after day. Not only this, but I actively became more flexible with my time so that I could attend to Michael's needs. During the same period, I finished my Master's degree in Education and was able to secure a much better job. This helped me to better provide for my son better. I further decided to cut down on the time that I invested in my real-estate business. It was a hard decision, but I never compromise when it comes to my children's needs. As I mentioned earlier, I will always put their needs and well-being in front of my own. Since I no longer had to devote a significant chunk of my day towards my real-estate business, I could direct all the spare time towards Michael. Making sure he got whatever he wanted, tending to his needs, and just being there for him.

In hindsight, I could not have made a better decision. As the year progressed, I could observe Michael's physical and emotional health getting better by the day. Apart from going to his school, Michael spent most of his time at home, but his mental state still continued to show significant progress.

Nonetheless, I continued driving Michael to his therapist as I did not want him to relapse into his depression. Additionally, to make sure that Michael felt comfortable sharing his struggles with me, I used to drive him to various activities that were spread out around Virginia. Not only did that allow Michael a distraction from his depression and put his mind elsewhere, doing something fun and productive, but it also strengthened the bond he shared with me.

Michael had started to be more open with me, and I no longer had to prod him to know the things that were going on in his life. He began to share things without me asking. He would talk about his day, even the dreams he had the night before. All in all, Michael's continued to become better; he was recovering like the champion he was. He was becoming happier by the day, and I was so proud to see him fight his depression.

One day, suddenly, I received a call from the university Michael had planned to attend after graduating. They informed me that Michael had successfully passed their admission test as well as the final interview and had secured an esteemed position in their college. I was so excited for my boy. After the call, I couldn't control my happiness.

Tears of joy kept rolling down my cheeks as I began to imagine seeing my boy attend the prestigious university and hopefully start afresh. I was so grateful to God for giving this to him. I knew how much it meant to Michael to get into a college of his own choice and caliber. I immediately ran into Michael's room and embraced him tightly. Since his childhood, Michael had always dreamt of becoming a doctor, and seeing him get closer to his dream made the two of us so happy.

A few days later, I took Michael to the university and enrolled him in a few biology courses. Despite my happiness, somewhere in my heart, I still felt that Michael would not be able to deal with the pressure that came with university life. Especially considering the difficult courses, he had to take up to eventually get enrolled in med school.

Regardless, I remained hopeful, and I continued praying to God. I knew my son was strong, he had shown life he was worthy of living twice, and I hoped he only grew stronger from that day. After completing his first semester at the university, Michael informed me that he no longer wanted to go back and continue his studies. At the time, I felt a little disappointed, it was sad to see my boy give up on his dreams like that, but I snapped myself out of my selfish thoughts and felt relieved that my son had finally started opening up about his feelings with me.

I was so glad he trusted me enough to share this important news. He further told me that the stress that came with his academics was gradually getting worse, and he could sense his depression creeping back into his life. I remember holding his hand tightly and telling him that it is okay and that whatever decision he takes for himself will be final. I told him that he no longer has to continue with his studies if he does not feel like it, and as discussed, Michael dropped out of his university, and since then has never gone back to school.

Unfortunately, it was too late. Even though Michael had discontinued his studies and he no longer had to deal with any sort of academic pressure, all of the progress Michael had made before joining the university appeared to have gone down the drain. His depression overtook him, and his health continued to get worse by the day.

His doctor informed me that Michael's medications needed to be adjusted, and, as such, my son was once again forced to make routine trips to the hospital. Once again, I stopped eating and sleeping. I felt so tired and exhausted. I kept thinking about what went wrong in our lives that we continuously face these obstacles along the way. In contrast, Pol, his father continued to blow his money on drinking and gambling. Every night, he returned home, reeking of another woman's perfume.

One day, after Pol returned home, I immediately hugged him. In hindsight, I think that, at the time, I felt so desperate and hopeless due to Michael's declining health that I tried to seek comfort in Pol's arms. I had no one to go to, no one to share the mental and emotional trauma that I had been holding inside of me for the past few months.

I couldn't help but find myself in Pol's arms— someone who I once loved and cared for. He couldn't help but ask me why I was acting affectionate towards him. I told him that I was terrified of losing him, but I did not believe that he could change by himself. For some odd reason, my comment infuriated Pol, and he pushed me away; his hands did not exert a lot of force at me, but they were enough to let me know what he was going to say next.

As I had feared, Pol suddenly raised his voice and started screaming at me, saying that he did not need to change as he was not doing anything wrong. In his anger, he began to justify all of his questionable actions by telling me that he was not an alcoholic even though he drank. He said that he worked day and night for all of us and that it is only fair if he gambles his money away sometimes.

Unfortunately, that was not the entire truth. Pol did not support the household with his salary at all. He would instead frequently go to the casinos gambling away whatever little money he earned. Whenever he would lose his money, he would start nagging me to loan him some cash. What's worse is that Pol, without any shame whatsoever, even admitted that he regularly dated women other than me.

He justified his unfaithful and toxic behavior by telling me that he was not serious with them. He was not only using and exploiting me but was doing the same with countless other women. In his tantrum, he yelled that no one could ever change him, and, instead of badgering him, I should stay at home and take care of him and the children. Pol accused me of smothering him and told me that he deserved to have fun in his life.

Before leaving me alone in the room, he gave me an ultimatum: either I should get used to his behavior or leave him alone. After hearing all that Pol had to say, despite me opening up to him, sharing with him that a part of me still cared for him, I could feel all the hope that I had managed to retain for my marriage seep away from my body. A few days later, something very unfortunate happened that finally made me consider filing for a divorce.

Michael was not feeling well, so I admitted him to the psychiatric ward before returning home. Pol's whereabouts were unknown as usual. Around 2 AM, I received a call from one of my friends who lived in

New York. I had not heard from her in so many years, and I found it quite strange that she was calling me late in the night.

Nonetheless, I managed to answer the phone, thinking that there might be an emergency. After some formal greetings, she informed me that she was in town with her husband to visit some distant relatives. On their way back, they spotted Pol in his car, and it seemed like he had been in an accident.

At first, they thought of stopping their car and helping him, but when they saw another woman in the passenger seat, they drove off, thinking that it was someone else. They told me that the lady in Pol's car resembled a young, American girl. Before hanging up the call, I thanked my friends for telling me what they had seen.

The strange thing was, I tried to call them back to tell them what had happened, but the phone was disconnected. How could it be, they just called an hour ago and it was 2:00 A.M. Since then, I had not heard from them again. Immediately, I got out of bed, covered myself up with my robe, and drove to the place my friend mentioned, but there was no sign of an accident there. However, there was a restaurant nearby, and, from the outside, it appeared to be full of people.

When I moved closer to the restaurant's window, I saw Pol sitting at a booth along with three other people. A white girl who matched my friends' description was seated next to him with another couple sitting opposite to them. I can still recall how I felt at that instant; my heart seemed to be pounding against my ribcage, and time itself appeared to have slowed down. I don't know what brought me to make that decision, but I somehow, with no rational thought whatsoever, walked towards the door of the busy restaurant. The fluorescent lights flashed in my eyes as I stepped in. I felt so out of place, I had no idea what I was doing, but before I knew it, I found myself in front of Pol's table.

I tapped him gently on his shoulder and told him about Michael's health. I requested him to come home as he was very sick and his presence would mean a lot to him. Pol, however, shamelessly ignored me and continued laughing at a story that one of the people at his table was narrating. I felt humiliated, but more than that, I was infuriated.

A wave of rage took over my body, and I snatched the beer bottle Pol was holding in his hand and smashed it on the table. "Your son is in the hospital! Can you hear me?" I yelled at him. Everyone around me started staring at Pol before the restaurant manager came out and asked us to leave.

In my rage, I rightly decided that I did not want to live with such a heartless and selfish man anymore. It was at that moment when I realized I had to liberate myself from this painful and loveless marriage. As I mentioned earlier, whatever happens, happens for a reason, and this whole incident was carefully orchestrated by God to make me realize that I was trapped in this marriage, that I was wasting away my days hoping I could mend this lost bond that we once shared.

I hurried towards my car and raced home. I rushed into my home, walked up the stairs and pulled my bags and suitcases out of the closet, and started packing whatever things of mine I could get my hands on, but then I heard the sound of Pol's car approaching the driveway. Suddenly, dread possessed me, and I did not open the door to our house; I just couldn't. I knew I humiliated Pol in front of his friends, and he couldn't have taken that lightly at all.

He kept banging on the front door, but I didn't move a muscle. A few minutes later, I heard the glass of the back door breaking. Pol had found a rock and broken the back-door to get inside the house. Thankfully, I kept my wits about myself, and I immediately ran out of the front door to my car and drove to my sister's house, who lived just one block away. I kept knocking at her door until she came out. I could not tell her the entire story and just begged her to let me stay at her house. She couldn't make sense of what was happening but was aware of what a terrible person Pol was. She, too, felt scared of Pol and went inside to discuss the matter with her husband. I waited outside, and when she didn't come back, I left.

I knew that the first place that Pol would search to find me would be my sister's house, and, as such, I entered my car and decided to look for another place to stay. I couldn't endanger their peace; it was too much of a burden to carry. I kept driving for a few miles before I finally pulled up outside a one-story brick house. When I knocked at the door, an older woman came out. I told her that I needed a place to stay, and I couldn't help but shed tears in front of her. I requested her to let me in, or else my husband would kill me. I was shaking with fear, and she could see that.

She let me inside and informed me that the home was a Samaritan House for Battered Women. However, there was no one other than the old lady inside the home. She gave me papers to sign before escorting me upstairs to a room that I would sleep in for the night. I asked her if there was anyone else living there, and she did not reply. I started feeling uneasy, but I had nowhere else to go.

On the upper floor, two bedrooms were situated next to each other, and I immediately locked myself in the room in which I was supposed to stay. I felt so fearful that I even pushed a big chest of drawers against the room's door so that no one could get inside even if they tried to get in. Moreover, I began thinking of an escape plan in case something went wrong. I saw that there was a window in the room, and I decided that I would jump out of it if someone were to enter my room.

I immediately took out my rosary and started praying, weeping to God for His support. I knew I was nothing without Him and could only turn to Him for any kind of help. Suddenly, there were loud bangs at the door, and I heard the lady's voice shouting angrily at me. I got scared, and I didn't know what to say or do. As I came to find out, the poor old soul had schizophrenia and was hallucinating. At the time, I felt immensely nervous. I continued chanting my prayers as I stepped out of my room and began making my way down the stairs.

I had just descended a single step when I noticed that the old lady was standing at the bottom of the stairs. She kept staring at me for a few seconds before suddenly yelling at me. Suddenly, out of the blue, calm overtook me, and I placed my trust in God.

It was help from Him. He had responded to my prayers and had blessed me with the strength to gather my wits and face yet another obstacle life shot at me. I politely inquired the old lady about her name, and she responded. I showed her the rosary in my hand, and I told her how I always kept it by my side. As I was talking, I started making my way down the stairs. When I reached the middle of the stairway, I stopped, and I calmly asked the lady, "Do you know how to pray, and would you like to pray with me? I will teach you how to."

The middle-aged lady didn't utter a single word in response. When I reached closer to her, I showed her the rosary before letting her touch it. At this point, she seemed to have calmed down. We sat together on one of the steps, and I taught her the Our Father prayer, also called the Lord's Prayer.

Tears began to roll down the woman's cheeks, and when I asked her why she was crying, the poor soul told me how she had ended up near Virginia Beach, even though she was originally from New York. When she seemed to have somewhat calmed down, I informed her that I needed to leave because my son was admitted to the hospital. Before I could go, she handed me one of her pictures and requested me to pray for her.

I promised her that I would always keep her in my prayers, and I ran as fast as I could out the door to my car. I managed to find myself at a friend's house and spent the next few nights with her. I did not want to burden my friend's family, and, therefore, I decided to eventually find a place where I could live on my own in peace. I ended up renting a home near the water, and after a year had passed, I was able to save up enough to purchase a condo and started living there. Meanwhile, before I decided to divorce Pol, I quit my teaching job. I renewed my license in Real Estate, and I continued with my Real Estate business. I also bought a new condo near the ocean. In retrospect, I could have lived happily in my new place. Since Michael was stuck with his dad, I lived by myself. I could not call Michael, and I could not see him. I missed him so dearly, and my heart ached whenever I thought of him. Unfortunately, I could not do anything at the time, and I just put him in God's hands.

My husband didn't get over his disgusting habits. He continued his drinking, kept sleeping with other women, and kept gambling away all of his savings. He was a complete mess. I decided to hire a private investigator to follow him as I needed proof to have peace of mind. I wanted to make sure that I was making the right call in divorcing him. A part of me still somehow hoped things could get better, I guess. I was tired of his lies, all those fights, and sleepless nights. I was tired of worrying about catching AIDS and various other hurtful emotions.

The investigator I had hired sent me some pictures, but I still wasn't fully convinced that I was making the right call by divorcing Pol. It was not the investigator's fault after all, as he could not enter bedrooms in motels just to take pictures.

All this time, I continued to live by myself. I missed my children so much; I missed seeing them laugh, and I missed holding them tightly in my embrace every day. Pol, with his poor habits, continued to move from one place to another, so I could not trace Michael. Until one day, a friend of mine called me unexpectedly; she lived nearby Pol's new apartment. She recognized my son, Michael, who was talking to some police officers in front of her yard. The neighbors filed a complaint that Michael was always sleeping in their front yard late at night. I drove hurriedly to the address. But, by the time I arrived, everybody was gone. I didn't know where to find Michael.

One day, I decided to make an unexpected visit to their apartment, hoping that Pol would not be at home. I saw Michael talking with an older American woman. I didn't ask if she was his girlfriend. Michael didn't introduce me to her, and both of them seemed to not care. While they were busy talking in the front yard, I sneaked into Pol's place. The door was unlocked, so I quietly went inside. Pol was not home, and it was already very late at night. When I heard footsteps coming towards the door, I immediately laid down on the couch and covered myself with the sofa cover. At first, I thought it was Pol, but it was Michael and the old lady. She sat on the empty seat opposite where I was, and she laid back down. Michael went to his room, and I heard him close the door behind him.

Soon after, I heard someone open the door, and it was Pol walking in. He went towards the lady and kissed her. The entire area was dark. The only light on in the living room was the light coming in from the streets. Thankfully, he didn't check who it was under the covered sheet. He probably assumed it was Michael. Pol and the lady went into the bedroom and locked the door behind them. I just waited until they got settled, then rushed out of the house and into my car. I didn't have the time to talk to Michael. I was so upset about seeing my son being neglected like that.

He gained so much weight and looked very untidy. Soon after that incident, I filed for guardianship so that Pol could not take Michael away from me. Thankfully, the court granted me Michael's custody, and both of us started living in the condo I had bought the previous year. Moreover, I filed a restraining order against Pol to ensure the safety of my children. To be perfectly candid, I cannot recall how I felt after Pol and I divorced. I just remember an overwhelming sense of peace and calm that engulfed me and my children's lives. I was finally free.

8

There is an appointed time for everything and a time
for every affair under the heavens. Ecclesiastes 3:1

Peace At Last

My decision to separate from Pol came as a surprise to everyone in my life, including Pol. After all, we had been married for 36 years, and people often perceived our marriage to be the ideal example of a functional marriage. However, none of them had any insight regarding the emotional and physical distress that I had to endure during those 36 years. When I had filed for divorce, even Pol could not help but be astounded by my decision. He had thought that I could never muster up enough courage to separate from him, especially since we had been together for almost four decades. If I am sincere, I do not regret my decision to divorce him at all. When we had been together, I had talked to Pol on many occasions, begging him to change for the sake of our marriage and our children.

But Pol had always been an incredibly stubborn person, even when he was in the wrong. Whenever I communicated my concerns to Pol, he always said that nobody, including our children and me, could change his toxic personality. Pol, in his delirium, believed that he was too angelic to do anything wrong and that I was just a nagging wife who had nothing better to do. Now that I think about all our fights, I cannot help but laugh at his stupid comments. He often told me that I should feel privileged to have been married to a man like him; unfortunately, all I felt was distressed and contained.

By the time I decided to change my life and divorce Pol, I had already suffered so much due to his spiteful attitude, and the only thing I wanted was peace. After the divorce was granted in 2004, Pol went crazy. Almost every day, he used to follow me whenever I left for works. Some days, he would end up chasing me to the highways. I distinctly remember one instance where I pulled over my car to confront Pol for his stalkerish behavior. When I screamed at him to leave me alone, Pol pushed me towards the ditch that bordered the highway; at that instant, I saw my life flashing before my eyes. Thankfully, I managed to retain my wits and immediately got inside my car before speeding towards my job. Even my coworkers began to feel scared of Pol as he would often wait for me outside my office. One day, some of my friends at my job got so scared that they requested the secretary to contact the police. After that incident, I filed a restraining order against Pol, and things gradually started to get better.

Now that I no longer had to worry about facing any disappointment and hurt from Pol, I decided to focus my attention on Michael's health and well-being. When Michael was admitted to the hospital, he met another patient staying in the ward next to him. Over time, they became very close friends. To be honest, I never really appreciated the tone in which she used to talk to Michael. Perhaps my maternal instinct forced me to be skeptical about the girl's intentions as I did not want Michael to suffer again. Regardless, my instincts proved themselves to be right.

Within a few months of their friendship, Michael had fallen heads over heels in love with the girl. Immediately after getting discharged from the hospital, Michael and the girl went to a judge and got married. At the time, I could not believe it when I heard that Michael had taken such a significant step in his life without consulting me. I felt hurt and overlooked, and I began thinking that Michael was reverting back to his old habits of keeping things to himself.

Nonetheless, I pushed myself to be happy for Michael because the marriage had brought about a positive change in his personality, at least for a brief period. I did not see Michael for some time, and I began feeling more and more anxious every day.

However, I consoled myself by thinking that, perhaps, Michael and her bride were in the honeymoon phase of their marriage. Sadly, I could not have been more wrong. Finally, a few months after their wedding, I received a call from Michael's wife, who told me that she needed my help. Apparently, both Michael and his wife did not have any proper jobs and, therefore, could not afford a place to live.

After the call ended, I remember falling back on the couch in my living room. The conversation with Michael's wife made me realize that one of my biggest fears had come true. At the time, I remember wishing that Michael had told me about his decision to elope with the girl he had met when he was admitted to the mental institution. I would have immediately advised him to take some time to ponder over his thoughts and not to rush into anything impulsively. After all, both Michael and the girl were going through a rough period in their lives; not only were they suffering from a mosaic of mental illnesses, but neither of them could secure a stable source of income. Unfortunately, Michael did not think that my advice was necessary, and, now, he and his wife were homeless.

I also felt incredibly guilty the day I received the call from Michael's wife. My inner voice kept forcing me into thinking that I had been a horrible mother, and that must have been why Michael did not inform me that he was about to get married. Regardless, Michael needed my help, and, as I have mentioned multiple times throughout this book, I do not rely on fate when it comes to my boys' well-being. That day, I rented out a room in a nearby motel for Michael and his wife, and they ended up staying there for several days. I also give them allowances so they could afford groceries and other essentials. During those days, I could not help but be sad and happy at the same time. I was pleased because I could financially support my son and his wife, but what made me sad was that they needed my help in my first place.

A few days later, Michael and his wife moved out of the motel to live with the latter's parents. After that, I could not see Michael for almost three years as they did not have a permanent address and hopped around from place to place. During this period, Michael had also started neglecting his medicines because he could not afford them, and, as such, his mental health had started to deteriorate again steadily. To this day, I believe that those three years were one of the most challenging phases of my life. After all, I could not see my son, and he, in turn, was unable to resort to his mother for any sort of help.

One day, out of the blue, I received a call from Michael's wife. When I realized that it was her, I immediately felt a storm of emotions breeze through me. I was angry that they had not bothered to reach out to me in three years, and I wanted to reprimand them for that. At the same time, I felt glad that at least I knew that they were alive. However, in a matter of minutes, all my feelings were replaced by a single emotion: dread.

Michael's wife informed me that she had cheated on Michael and gotten pregnant with another man. Before I could comprehend her statement, I was told that Michael would return to my house to live with me. My heart sank to my stomach. A sense of dread enveloped me as I began thinking about what Michael must have been feeling when he found out that his wife had been unfaithful to him. I was petrified that Michael might make another attempt at his life.

When Michael finally arrived at my doorsteps, he was sick, motionless, and hurt. I quickly took him inside to my living room and embraced him. Even though he had multiple emotional wounds, my son had finally become reunited with his mother. I comforted him by telling him that whatever had happened, it had happened for the best, and now, at least he had realized the real character of his wife. Additionally, upon Michael's consent, I called his wife and told her that Michael wanted a divorce. She did not object, and Michael and I contacted a judge. A short time later, I paid the judge, and the divorce was finalized. Ever since then, Michael has not seen his ex-wife.

I am delighted to say that Michael has really turned his life around after separating from his wife. Sure, like every other person, he too has bad days and good days, but, thankfully, his old ambitious self has slowly started coming back. Every day, he seems better and better, and I cannot begin to describe the happiness I feel whenever I see him smiling. For such a long time,

Michael only seemed depressed and hopeless. Even when he laughed or smiled, my maternal instincts knew that he was faking his happiness. But now, his smile seems more genuine than ever, and I cannot thank God enough for helping my beautiful baby boy.

While all of this had been going on, Pol continued to make my life a living hell. Owing to his chronic drinking, he was once caught by the cops while driving under the influence of alcohol. He was charged with a DUI, and the judge sent him to prison. From there, he called me and begged me to free him by paying for his bail. He made innumerable promises about becoming a better man, and, feeling incredibly pitiful, I did settle his bail.

After he was released, he once again contacted me and asked me to loan him some money to pay his rent. Once again, I could not help but feel pity for him, and I ended up giving him some money. Even though we were divorced, I still kept doing things for him out of my stupidity. After all, we had been married for 36 years, and I felt incredibly sorry for him, but I also knew I had to be resilient. I was stuck between a rock and a hard place.

On the one hand, I hated Pol for all the hurt and misery he had caused to our sons and me; however, on the other hand, I wanted to help him since he was the father of my children, and I just could not let him ruin his life, something he was exceptionally skilled at doing. At times, a similar thought kept manifesting itself in my mind. It prodded me into thinking that Pol might change after the divorce and that he might come to understand the real importance of my children and me. If that had been the case, I might have actually taken him back, provided that he demonstrated his intentions to be sincere. Something deep down in my heart kept telling me that I was capable of forgiving him. Perhaps, everything I was feeling was the only natural. For 36 years, I had lived with him. Even though I hate admitting it, I had also become emotionally dependent on him.

How could I not? Before our divorce, I really loved him and, whenever he caused me any hurt, I deluded myself into thinking that he would change just like I had begun to do after our separation. In my opinion, the divorce had brought about a radical shift in my life, and I was having a hard time keeping up with it. Perhaps, that is why I subtly hoped that Pol would become turn over a new leaf. Had that been the case, I shiver to think that I might have actually acquitted Pol for everything he had done and remarried him. At the same time, I believe that even if I had taken Pol back, he would have continued with his old habits of drinking, gambling, and dating other women. Regardless of my thoughts, Pol never changed; in his own words, nothing could make him change.

After our divorce, Pol left Virginia to go live in the Philippines. Rather than starting anew, Pol continued to do terrible things in his new country. He could easily afford to do his addictions in the Philippines due to their low prices. After a year of living in the Philippines, Pol informed one of our mutual friends that he had become a baby girl's father. Then, almost another year later, he once again became the father of a baby boy. At the time, I had assumed that maybe he had gotten the same woman pregnant twice. However, knowing Pol, I should have thought better. Not only he had gotten two separate women pregnant, but the mother of his new-born son had already been married to someone else.

When I heard all of this, I felt incredibly thankful that I did not take Pol back. Just like I had assumed, Pol continued with his disgusting unfaithfulness even after our divorce, although, this time around, I was not the victim of his infidelity, I digress. Owing to the funds he received after retiring from the navy and his social security pension, Pol was living a life of luxury in the Philippines. Moreover, he was able to afford himself a house. As far as I know, he is not living with anyone. Perhaps, the women he got pregnant with also realized his ugly character and decided to leave him. Pol is also financially supporting one of his new children: the baby girl.

His daughter is a gem to him. I know this because Pol told our mutual friends that the only reason he was not happy with me was that I could not give him a daughter, and now that he has one, he is finally happy. To be completely candid, I feel glad that he has yet found a purpose in his life: his daughter. Even though I will never entirely forgive him for making my life and my children's lives a nightmare, I hope that he too finds real happiness, the kind of joy I have uncovered ever since our separation.

9

Return to the stronghold—you prisoners of hope.

Even today, I declare That I will restore double to

you. Zechariah 9:12

Paul becomes a Business Owner!

With all the desolations, problems, trials, sadness, guilt, disappointment, and pain following me, I forgot that I needed to take care of my eldest son: Paul. Since I had been so occupied taking care of Michael, I did not notice that Paul's emotional needs were being disregarded. But after the divorce and Michael's recovery, I realized that, during all this time, I had not been paying due attention to Paul. Once again, I could feel my heart spasming out of guilt.

Paul lived with us until he finished his four-year college degree at Virginia Tech and graduated from Wesleyan College. Like every other fresh graduate, Paul had no idea what sort of career path he wanted to pursue. I, too, did not pressure him into getting a job. My readers might think that since I did not push Paul to search for a career path, I was a bad mother, but that is not the whole picture. Two reasons made me reluctant whenever I thought of having a conversation with Paul regarding his future. Firstly, Paul did not seem very serious about finding a job.

After his graduation, he had worked numerous odd jobs that paid him minimum wage. At the time, Paul seemed happy with whatever little he was earning and did not ask me for money. However, after a couple of months, he quit his job and began spending most of his time at home. I would be lying if I said that I did not worry about his future. To this day, I worry about both my sons' lives even though they are happy and satisfied. The second reason that stopped me from pressuring Paul about his professional life was that I feared that, due to the added stress, his emotional well-being might decline just like Michael's had. After all, the sole reason behind Michael's turbulent health was the stress and anxiety he had been feeling because of his academics and home-life. Every day, Michael would arrive home from school just to see his father berating his mother or vice versa.

I feared that if I nagged Paul about finding a full-time job, he might devolve into the same mental state as Michael, especially since his brother was already going through an incredibly turbulent time of his life. These two reasons collectively convinced me to let Paul shape his future, and, instead of continually badgering him, I patiently waited for Paul to realize his ambitions.

Surprisingly, my strategy worked. One day, Paul informed me that he wanted to have a serious discussion with me. Considering that I already felt guilty about ignoring his needs for such a long time, I happily obliged Paul's request. That day, after we were done having dinner, Paul and I sat together in the living room. I calmly waited for him to disclose whatever he wanted to talk to me about, and, after a few seconds of palpable silence, he did.

Drawing a tentative breath, Paul informed me that he needed money to buy a plane-ticket for California. He and his friend wanted to take the entrance exam for Cleveland Chiropractic School in Los Angeles,

California. Even though his revelation took me by surprise, I felt a great deal of contentment, knowing that my son was finally working towards actualizing his ambitions. The next day, I paid him the full amount for the plane-ticket, and, a few days later, he and his friend ended up flying to California.

Initially, I had thought that Paul would immediately return home after taking the entrance exam. However, that was not the case. Ever since he was a kid, Paul always loved the beach. Whenever we went to the beach, he would spend hours swimming in the ocean. One of the reasons Paul had an innate affinity with the ocean was because he loved surfing. In California, too, he fell in love with the water. One day, out of the blue, I received a call from Paul. I was utterly shocked to hear that Paul wanted to stay in California. When I inquired him about his friend who had accompanied Paul to the entrance test, Paul informed me that he had already left for his home in Virginia. Sure enough, his friend returned to his home a few days later, and Paul was not on the plane with him. At the time, Paul's decision to stay in California saddened me. More than that, it made me anxious about my son's safety.

All of these events had transpired in 2004. Even though we would regularly talk with each other, I still could not help but think about Paul. One day, I decided to surprise him. I bought a plane ticket to California and flew there to find him. Thankfully, he was safe and secure when I finally stumbled upon him. This time, I realized that I needed to ask Paul what he wanted to do with his life. In response, Paul divulged to me that he wanted to become a chiropractor. As such, I took him to a chiropractor college and enrolled him there. I also found a place for him to live near his college and paid for his rent. After I had finished putting together everything he needed, I bid farewell to Paul and flew back to my home in Virginia. During my flight back home, I started feeling incredibly anxious about Paul.

After all, he did not know anyone in the area, and he was utterly alone. There were nights where I could not sleep, as I would feel apprehensive about Paul. If he were to get sick, there would be no friends or family members that could take care of him. Nonetheless, I trusted my gut that he would be alright. Once in a while, I used to call Paul and talk to him about his life. Paul completed his doctorate in 2010. I, his dad, and Michael attended his convocation. At the time, I could not have been any more proud of him. Despite all the difficulties he had to face throughout his life, including his parents' divorce and Michael's sickness, Paul had managed to graduate with flying colors. At his graduation ceremony, we did not discuss if Paul would be returning home.

Neither Paul mentioned anything about coming back to Virginia, nor did I invite him. After all, it was his big day, and I did not want to bother him with trivial matters. His graduation had shown me that I could trust Paul with every decision he makes in his life. Nonetheless, Paul's journey towards his graduation was not a smooth ride, as there were quite a few interruptions. A few months after he had started attending college, Paul also started working as a bartender. He informed me that he did not want to complete his schooling since he could earn more money in tips from his bartending than his friends, who were all chiropractors.

Once again, I made my way over to his home in California and talked to him. Due to my persistence, Paul finally agreed to go back to his college, and I returned home happier than I had thought I would be. In 2008, two years before his graduation, Paul found a job in a chiropractic office in Los Angeles, where he worked till 2014.

During his stay in Los Angeles, Paul had to face quite a few problems. He did not inform me about any of them because if I had been aware of his trials, I would have immediately rushed there to help him. Perhaps, one of the reasons Paul kept his tribulations to himself was that I was already incredibly occupied in taking care of Michael's deteriorating health during those months.

He must not have wanted to bother me. Once, while having a conversation with me, Paul informed me that he had to live in his car at one point during his time in California. However, due to his determination and resilience, Paul overcame all the problems dragging him down. Every time he subdued his adversities, his courage and tenacity mounted.

If I am honest, I am incredibly proud of Paul. Not only did he end up learning quite a few significant lessons during his stay in California, but he also found his true potential there. As I mentioned earlier, in 2014, Paul worked in a chiropractic office in Los Angeles. However, his boss was quite a vicious person. There were times when his boss would hold back his salary, and, consequently, Paul had to work quite a few odd jobs along with his regular full-time one.

I recall an instance when I called Paul, and he informed me that he was working as a model in a department store in Los Angeles. I was quite surprised to hear that, but Paul assured me that he did not need any help. In fact, now that I think of it, I have never heard Paul complain about anything. Whenever I used to call him, he would sound excessively enthusiastic, and I could not tell that he had been struggling. Never once did Paul request me for any sort of financial help either. That is just how Paul has been ever since he was a child. He would instead figure things out himself than asking anyone for support.

In 2015, Paul stumbled across an office with a sign placed outside it that read: For rent. That very day, I received a call from Paul. Paul told me that he wanted to take me somewhere, and I agreed to his request. The next day, Paul and I drove to the office that was for rent. Paul parked the car across from the building, and he just sat there silently. Neither did Paul let me leave the car, nor did he show me the offices' inside. When I asked him if everything was alright, Paul politely asked me if I could lend him $4000. When I inquired him about the reason for asking for such a considerable sum of money, Paul informed me that he wanted to rent one of the offices inside the building. Keeping in mind that Paul had never broken my trust before, I agreed to lend him the money. Almost a week later, we drove to the same building again.

Paul informed me that he needed $4000 more to rent the office next to the one he had rented a week prior as it was also being vacated. This time though, Paul did tell me that he intended on starting his own business venture; however, he refrained from mentioning what kind of business he would be opening. He also did not show me any sort of documentation about the company he had intended on opening. Nonetheless, as I mentioned earlier, ever since his graduation, I had come to trust Paul in all of his decisions. As such, I lent him another $4000 and blessed him. After Paul had rented both the offices, it was time for me to fly back to Virginia. For quite an extended period, I did not hear anything from Paul.

Even when we talked to each other on call, we just inquired about each other's lives, and none of us ever mentioned anything about his business. In November of 2015, during one of our regular calls, Paul informed me that he had finally opened a chiropractic office with the money I had lent him. He also told me that he had hired eight employees. At the time, I felt strange. Do not get me wrong; I was incredibly excited that my son had finally actualized his ambitions.

Not only was I enthusiastic about this new chapter in his life, but I was also ready to help him again both financially and in any other way possible. However, at the same time, I felt a seed of doubt sprouting in my heart. I kept asking myself if Paul would be able to handle the stress that comes with operating a business.

After all, I, too, owned a restaurant back in the day, and I knew that managing a venture is not as easy as it sounds. Running a business comes with its own set of difficulties, and I did not want Paul to overburden himself. What exacerbated my doubts was that Paul had no prior experience in sales or marketing. Even though he had worked quite a few odd jobs before, none of them specifically required the skill set needed to manage a business. Nonetheless, I consoled myself by thinking that since Paul worked in a chiropractic office, he must have learned the ins and outs of operating a business venture. Whenever we talked on calls, I used to encourage and motivate him. At the same time, I regularly prayed to God to make things easier for my son. Once, Paul invited me to California to take a tour of his office.

When I arrived there, I made quite a few suggestions to help Paul run things more efficiently. However, I soon realized that Paul did not appreciate my criticisms. After all, he had invited me to see how far he had come in his life, and he had expected me to be proud of his accomplishments, not to demotivate his spirit. When I arrived back at my condo in Virginia, I realized that I had unintentionally hurt his feelings, but Paul did not mention anything like that. After a few months had passed, Paul called me and invited me once again to his office. This time, however, his offices had wholly changed. Not only did they give off a very professional vibe, but, most importantly, they had a very pleasing atmosphere and were kept very clean.

There were three rooms that Paul had purchased and rented with the $8000 I had loaned him, and all of them had proper equipment for specific needs. Paul had also hired eight employees, which included doctors, therapists, as well as his personal helpers and secretaries. Ever since he was a child, Paul always loved helping people. Whenever he managed to make someone's life easier, a big goofy smile would sweep across his handsome face. Now, he had finally achieved his lifelong dream of aiding others by becoming a chiropractor. When I was done touring his office, I felt tears forming in my eyes. After all, I was so incredibly proud of his determination and hard work. What makes me even happier is that he is finally satisfied with his life, and, like me, he too is immensely proud of all his achievements.

In 2017, Paul invited his brother and me to spend the Christmas holidays with him. When our flight landed, and we met him at the airport, Paul informed me that California was going to be my permanent home. At the time, I thought he was joking, but I could not have been more wrong. Paul told me that, previously, he could not afford to bring his brother and me out to California, but now that he can, he has a condominium for us. Paul drove Michael and me to the condo. I could not help but tear up at that moment, and I immediately embraced Paul. I could not believe what was happening.

Paul also said that it was time for me to retire and enjoy my life. He advised me to go traveling with my friends. After that, Paul drove me to his home. Even though it was quite expensive, it was also stunning, and I felt so proud thinking about how Paul had turned around his life. His house is only two blocks away from the condominium he has arranged for us. Even now, I have a hard time taking in the changes that have occurred in my life.

Back in Virginia, I had to wrap up all of my responsibilities so hurriedly that I did not even get the opportunity to say goodbye to my friends. Within two weeks, I had rented out my condo in Virginia Beach, Virginia, collected Michael's and my records from the doctor, and selected someone in my real-estate office to take care of my business while I was gone. Now I am back in California, living an incredibly unique life. It indeed has been an adventure, to say the least.

Bless the Lord, my soul; all my being, bless his holy

name! Bless the Lord, my soul; do not forget all the

gifts of God,

Who pardons all your sins, heals all your ills.

Psalm 103: 1-3

Towards a New Beginning

However, in the final chapter of my book, I must emphasize the role that faith played in my life-journey. There were numerous times when I was on the verge of giving up all hope, but then, at the very last second, I would often be subjected to a miraculous event that would rejuvenate my spirits. These events would indicate to me God had not abandoned me, and knowing that helped me immensely as I traversed through turbulent times in my life.

When I was still with Pol and was being forced to endure the hurt and suffering he would continually inflict on my children and me, I never once had a feeling of discontent that God was not around in the midst of my misery. I say so because I encountered his presence multiple times. One night, I was on my way to the local Church to attend a bible study responsible for organizing. I had just parked my car next to a nearby tree when a brilliant white light began emanating from the tree with the image of Jesus as a Shepherd. As I got closer to find out if it was real, the light disappeared as abruptly as it had appeared.

When I went inside the Church, I informed the pastor that I had just witnessed a sign from God. At first, I thought he would not believe me, but he advised me to keep what I had seen a secret when he noticed my alarmed demeanor.

He said that I might not be ready to divulge my experiences to someone else as my life was about to change radically. Since then, I have internalized the pastor's advice, and I never told anyone what I had been exposed to that day. However, whenever I pass by that tree when I am out to run an errand, I pray to God. I cannot come across that tree without that image of Jesus manifesting itself clearly in my mind.

The same year, I was invited by a friend to another church in the area where my house was located. I recall that Michael had been admitted to the hospital again that day, and I felt incredibly anxious about his mental and emotional well-being. As one can imagine, I had spent the entire day begging God to help my son. As I was on my way to the Church, I noticed an image of Jesus on a piece of cloth hanging on a wall. Immediately, tears began welling up in my eyes, and I inched closer to the wall to take in Jesus in all his glory. However, as soon as I got near it, the image disappeared. After a period of tentative deliberation, I finally decided to narrate what I had seen to my friends. I could not believe it when some of my friends informed me that they, too, had seen different images of God in that Church.

Additionally, my friends also revealed that whenever they had the privilege of witnessing one of God's innumerable miracles, they were on the verge of giving up all hope due to some challenges they were enduring in their lives.

When I heard that, I felt incredibly comforted. When I realized God himself had shown me a sign, I could not stop myself from crying. Not only did the experience rejuvenate my courage and hope, but I also returned to fighting the demons that were making a life a living hell at that time.

Similarly, I had a dream one night. I saw a giant man entering my bedroom, who then lovingly referred to me as his son. I felt petrified and woke up with my body covered in sweat. Out of my fear, I called a friend and narrated my dream to her. In response, she told me God himself had visited me in my dream.

A few months after this incident, I was helping out in the Church one day. I was in Los Angeles those days, and I actively used to attend a Church there. After mass, I was cleaning up the dust and mopping the floor when I noticed that the Blessed Mother had ribbons around her head. It was a weird image. After all, who would place ribbons around the head of the

Blessed Mother? The lady in charge of tending to the Church was present next to me. When I asked her who had placed the ribbons, she did not reply. She did not even turn her to look at the stature and continued working. After I had finished my work, I started searching for a ladder to help climb on and take the ribbons out of the Blessed Mother's head. Unfortunately, I was unable to locate a ladder anywhere in the Church.

The next day when I attended the mass, the ribbons were still there. I did not ask anyone else about it as I feared that they would start thinking that I was hallucinating. Eventually, the ribbons disappeared, but from then onwards, I started covering my head with a veil whenever I went inside a church as a sign of respect for the Blessed Mother and God. Moreover, I started observing the rules of the Church to pay respect to God. Ever since that experience, I never asked God to make my trials and tribulations go away in my prayers. Instead, I prayed for the Holy Spirit and Blessed Mother Mary to guide me whenever I had to make an essential decision for the sake of my children and me.

As one can imagine, God never let me down. In fact, I would say that God never lets anyone down. Not only is he good with his promises, but, most importantly, he always answers the prayers of his believers. These were not the only experiences I had with God. I am sure my readers might be wondering about my health. They might think that I never get sick. To answer their query, I must tell them that I do not have a perfect body. I also do believe in God's terms; we will die from sickness. However, God always cures the sicknesses and disorders that plague my body. As such, I never stop praying and believing in God's power. After all, my parents always told me that if one believes in God, he makes everything possible for them.

In 2013, I recall that I was scheduled to have knee surgery. I was in great pain and was unable to work or do anything for that matter. The only way I could move was with the help of a cane. The doctor has prescribed me a knee replacement as I had a tear in my meniscus. Two days before the surgery was scheduled to happen, I suddenly felt excellent. I no longer had an ache in my knee, and I was able to move around without any form of support. At the time, I could not believe it, but then, I remember what my parents always told me: anything is possible for God. That day, I went swimming with my friend to prove to her that I was not lying, that my knee did not hurt anymore.

Nonetheless, I once again visited the doctor and told him that I felt much better. He could not believe me when I told him that I felt no pain anymore. However, he, too, could not detect the tear in my meniscus again, and the surgery was canceled.

The following year, I noticed that I was bleeding. It went on for almost ten days, but I did not pay much attention to it as I did not feel any pain. I kept on doing my work when one of my friends finally forced me to go to the hospital. After inquiring about my symptoms, the doctor was not able to come up with a viable diagnosis. Nonetheless, he scheduled a blood transfusion for the next day. Surprisingly, all of my vital signs became normal the following day, and my bleeding also stopped.

The hospital asked me to perform numerous tests to underline the cause of the bleeding, but they could not provide a diagnosis. At the time, I had realized that a miracle had happened, and it was God himself who had helped me recover. I was admitted to the hospital for a week, after which the doctors discharged me as my physical health seemed perfectly okay. The blood transfusion never happened. Similarly, when I was in Los Angeles last year, I went for a mammogram at a UCLA facility to have my yearly check-up. The doctors informed me that they had detected a lump in my right breast. They told me that I needed to be monitored, and I was advised to return after six months for a second check-up. After my second check-up, my doctor told me that I should revisit the hospital after three months. When the doctor was about to take the biopsy on the day of my appointment, he could no longer detect the lump.

It seemed as if it had miraculously disappeared. I was sent home with a piece of happy news that day. The same year, a tremor in my brain was misdiagnosed by the doctors. All of these instances, I believe, are signs from God. I genuinely think that they are God's way of telling me that he is with me and that he will never abandon me in times of need.

I decided to dedicate the final chapter of my book to all of the times I have encountered God's miracles because I want my readers to understand that they are never alone. I want them to know that no matter what sort of problems they are facing in their lives, they should never ever lose their faith.

I say so because, from my own experiences, I can honestly say that God is with everyone. After all, he is the most beneficent. Had it not been for him, I would never have divorced Pol. It was God himself who guided me to separate from my ex-husband.

It was God who blessed Paul's business and cured Michael's illnesses. I want to end my book by saying that if God were not with me, I would not have been half as happy as I am today. Only because of him, my sons and I have finally learned what it means to be at peace. Thus, to all of my readers, always place your trust in God no matter how hard the circumstances surrounding you might get. I promise you that he would never let you down.

Inner Peace

Be courageous and religious. Have faith and pray

unceasingly!

AUTHOR'S BIO

Mila Gatchalian's life story is filled with a lot of captivating and engaging incidents. Mila Gatchalian wanted to write this story for a very long time and has now finally been able to shape all of her life experiences in this one enticing book.

Mila Gatchalian completed her B.S from The National Teachers College, Manila, Philippines, and her Master of Arts in Education from Regent University, Virginia Beach, Virginia.

She also earned a Graduate Degree in good standing from Sentara Mini-Medical School and Eastern Medical School, Norfolk, Virginia.

She is an esteemed member of the Circle of Excellence as well as an award winner awarded by the Hampton Roads Realtors Association, Virginia. She has also provided her services in the field of Real Estate and has been successful throughout her career.

She is also associated with Benedictine Oblate, which is affiliated with St. Vincent Archabbey, Latrobe, Pennsylvania.

Here & There Family Photos

Business Woman

My College Graduation

Paul Michael & Me

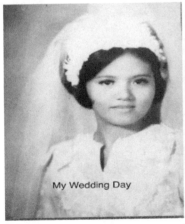
My first date and set up by Tita Pol

Michael and

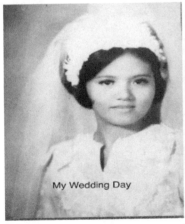

My Wedding Day

My grandma

My parents